I believe Ted Haggard's book, P
and compelling insights which will
has blessed Ted with the ability to ..ound things
simple and simple things profound.

Mike Bickle
Pastor, Metro Vineyard Fellowship
Kansas City, Missouri

Ted Haggard's witness is inspiring. Against the odds, regardless of the challenges, he helps us see the primary purpose for living. Invest in yourself. Enrich a life. Read this book.

Bishop Charles E. Blake
Minister, West Angeles Church of God in Christ
Los Angeles, California

As I have had the opportunity to observe Ted Haggard up close over the past three years, what has been clear is "this guy is for real." This book contains principles that are "for real." Reading it will encourage you, challenge you and make you a believer that all is not lost in the church nor the city as the millennial curtain drops upon the United States. More than that, the truths contained in *Primary Purpose* are transferable to any church in any city of the world.

Luis Bush
International Director, A.D. 2000 and Beyond Movement
Colorado Springs, Colorado

It's time to reach out to our communities and cities with the love and grace of Jesus Christ. Pastor Ted Haggard has been used of God in an extraordinary way to do just that. This book is filled with inspirational and practical insights on how we can minister to our communities. I encourage you to read it prayerfully and expectantly.

Paul Cedar
President, Evangelical Free Church of America
Minneapolis, Minnesota

Ted has written a powerful book desperately needed in this hour. It is about *people* — who need help. It is about *passion* — the love God has put in us. It is about *prayer* — getting in touch with God in a personal way. It is a *plan* for action — specific instructions on making a difference right now in the world where we live.

Billy Joe Daugherty
Pastor, Victory Christian Center
Tulsa, Oklahoma

Ted Haggard's *Primary Purpose* contains more practical insights on how believers can impact their communities for Christ than any book I've read. If you've prayed for practical steps to help see your community's spiritual climate change, *Primary Purpose* could well be the answer to that prayer.

Dick Eastman
International President, Every Home for Christ
Colorado Springs, Colorado

Reading Pastor Haggard's book helped me greatly to see more clearly how different we are in our approach to interpreting events and influences in our city. This leads me all the more to thank God for our friendship and mutual respect. By "concentrating on the absolutes," as he says, we are able to pray together and seek the Holy Spirit's wonderful works in our community as brothers in faith.

Bishop Richard D. Hanifen
Catholic Bishop of the Diocese of Colorado Springs

To my perspective, Ted Haggard is one of today's top ten rising spiritual leaders; a key man whose humility and practical yet sensitive style continue to cause me to want to listen to what Jesus is saying through him.

Jack Hayford
Senior Pastor, The Church on the Way
Van Nuys, California

Primary Purpose is one of the best how-to books I have ever read on how to change a city's spiritual climate. Pastor Haggard describes the Christian's primary purpose as that of making it hard for anyone to go to hell from our home towns and then gives us basic, biblical guidelines to accomplish that mission.

Throughout the book, he also highlights our Christian responsibility as one of praying for our cities as though it were a life-and-death matter — because it is! And by showing us how to engage in servant-minded spiritual warfare, he demonstrates how we can effectively communicate God's timeless message in a changing world to the glory of God.

Marilyn Hickey
Marilyn Hickey Ministries
Denver, Colorado

This book is a classic because it outlines the biblical foundation for uniting and mobilizing the church to reach our cities. Instead of a theory offered in a lecture hall, this is a proven experiment conducted in a laboratory with results that can be used in every community of the world. I commend this book to every person.

Jim Hylton
Senior Pastor, Lake County Baptist Church
Fort Worth, Texas

Primary Purpose is full of proven principles that will allow the church in a city to make a major impact on its community. It is written in a warm, intimate style that draws one closer to the Lord while planting the vision of capturing every man, woman and child in a city for the kingdom of God.

Cindy Jacobs
President, Generals of Intercession
Colorado Springs, Colorado

Colorado Springs has not been the same since Ted Haggard came to town. Its spiritual atmosphere has been charged by the strategies God has placed in Ted's heart. Here is a pastor who builds up all the other pastors in his city. Their unity has made Colorado Springs a spiritual lightning rod.

Terry Law
World Compassion/Terry Law Ministries
Tulsa, Oklahoma

Ted Haggard — probably more than any other pastor I know — has a vision which embraces a whole city, not just a local church. Until I read his book, *Primary Purpose*, I wasn't fully aware of the impact his vision has made on the city of Colorado Springs. The results are absolutely phenomenal. You can be sure, this book is not just spiritual hype, but contains real, grassroots principles which, when applied, will work for any church in any community.

Don Meares
Senior Pastor, Evangel Church
Upper Marlboro, Maryland

Primary Purpose rightly challenges the nature of evangelicals' uncompromising cooperation. With his notable style of graciousness and unencumbered joy, Ted shares the paradigm and models which he has successfully tested in Colorado Springs. Despite my theological differences, I would offer this brother's engaging book not only as *must* reading to every evangelical leader, but perhaps even as *regular* reading.

David L. Melvin
Assistant to the President
National Association of Evangelicals
Carol Stream, Illinois

Primary Purpose presents power-packed, practical principles that provide the impetus for change in the spiritual, social, cultural and economic environment in our cities, towns and nations. I would highly recommend this work to all serious students of the Word of God and to every Christian leader desiring not just to maintain the status quo in his city, but also to impact his society with the view to bringing generational transformation in his context.

Dr. Myles Munroe
President, Bahamas Faith Ministries, International
Nassau, Bahamas

Given the recent explosive interest in church growth and spiritual warfare, it's nice to have someone remind us why it makes so much sense to pursue these activities. While strategy and methodology are important — and this book offers plenty of both — *Primary Purpose* is ultimately about rationales. And it should be. For if Ted Haggard's own experience tells us anything, it is that true success (the kind that lasts) must flow from a deep understanding of *why* we are doing what we are doing.

George Otis, Jr.
Founder and President, The Sentinel Group
Lynnwood, Washington

While respecting the scriptural viewpoints of others, Pastor Ted Haggard presents his own convictions on how to turn an individual or an entire city from life without God to Christ. His practice of fasting and prayer, sharing and living God's truth, and being true to himself while embracing other believers of differing traditions offer fresh insights on how to have intimacy with God and fruitfulness in serving Him.

David L. Rambo
President, The Christian and Missionary Alliance
Colorado Springs, Colorado

I have pastored alongside and known Ted and Gayle Haggard for fifteen years. Their wisdom, integrity and compassion for the lost were pivotal in the radical transformation of Colorado Springs. *Primary Purpose* shows believers how to demolish every "high thought" so that our churches can pray, unite and harvest together.

Larry Stockstill
Senior Pastor, Bethany World Prayer Center
Baker, Louisiana

Many of us have been praying that our cities would be visibly changed by the power of God. *Primary Purpose* will 1) build your faith to know it can be done, and 2) give you practical steps to see a new spiritual climate come to your community.

C. Peter Wagner
President, Global Harvest Ministries
Pasadena, California

I wish *Primary Purpose* were required reading for every seminarian, Christian volunteer, church staff member, Bible school student and missionary. The practical tips on spiritual warfare, missions, loving and showing generosity toward other pastors and churches—these demonstrations of the kingdom of God are desperately needed today.

Doris Wagner
Executive Director, Global Harvest Ministries

Colorado Springs is not the same city that it was a few years ago. Families are drawn to a new gold rush of family values and spiritual peace in the community. Legislation did not make it possible, but a concentrated effort of local churches did. As a pastor, Ted's new book, *Primary Purpose*, inspires me to do more in my city. I know it will do the same for you.

Bob Yandian
Pastor, Grace Fellowship
Tulsa, Oklahoma

foreword by C. Peter Wagner

Primary

Purpose

Making It Hard for People to Go to Hell From Your City

TED HAGGARD

CREATION HOUSE
BOOKS ABOUT SPIRIT-LED LIVING
ORLANDO, FLORIDA

Creation House
Strang Communications Company
600 Rinehart Road
Lake Mary, FL 32746
Phone: 407-333-3132
Fax: 407-333-7100
Web site: http://www.strang.com

First printing, April 1995
Second printing, May 1995
Third printing, August 1995
Fourth printing, November 1995
Fifth printing, April 1996
Sixth printing, August 1996
Seventh printing, October 1996

Dedication

I owe many of the principles in this book to the influence of a great man, Pastor Roy Stockstill (affectionately known as Brother Roy) of Bethany World Prayer Center in Baker, Louisiana.

The first time I met Brother Roy, I had driven up to Bethany to make an appointment with him. As I pulled into the parking lot, I noticed a man off to one side painting a fence. I stopped to ask him where I might find Pastor Roy Stockstill. He looked at me politely and said, "I am Roy Stockstill. May I help you?"

I was surprised, but I knew I needed to set up an appointment with him so I said, "What do I need to do to set up an appointment with you?"

He looked at me and replied graciously, as only a Southern brother can, "If you would like, you may set up an appointment with me by picking up a paintbrush and help-ing me paint this fence."

By watching Brother Roy's life, I learned many of the philosophies that make ministry a pleasure. Though many experienced pastors become tired, cynical, bitter or weary, Brother Roy found a series of secrets in ministry that cause him to be faithful, fun, life-giving and steadfast. His wisdom and keen insight cause those who are just beginning in min-istry, and those who have been extremely effective for the cause of Christ, to desire his counsel and prayers.

I believe God sovereignly placed me in a position to observe and learn from Brother Roy, and those lessons have paved the way for steady ministry for me.

To this honorable man of God I humbly dedicate this work, knowing that his wisdom far surpasses the quality of ideas written here.

Toward the autumn years of my life, should God grant me the years of positive influence He has given Brother Roy, I would be very grateful.

Acknowledgments

Special thanks to those who labored together with me on this book.

First to my wife, Gayle, for her invaluable assistance in writing, editing and late-night rearranging. And to our very patient five children who heard about this book during birthday parties, picnics, baseball games, chores in the stables, Thanksgiving and Christmas celebrations, and every other family event for six months.

In addition I want to thank the wonderful people from New Life Church who encouraged me to write this book and allowed me to neglect returning their phone calls, cancel office appointments, and miss weddings and funerals in order to complete it.

And to our exceptional church staff who, under the competent leadership of Lance Coles, came to me and said they would assume additional responsibilities so I, Meg Britton (secretary) and Ross Parsley (associate pastor) could work as a team on this project. All of these friends sacrificed in order to allow the production of this book. Thank you.

And a grateful thanks to Deborah Poulalion, editor, for her sincere interest and determination to make me write; and the team from Strang Communications and Creation House. A warm thank-you to Lee Grady, Steve Strang, John Mason, Tom Freiling and Kelli Bass. And to Walter Walker, who was the first to encourage me to write these ideas in book form.

And finally, a heart-felt thank you to my parents, the late Dr. J. Marcus Haggard and my mother, Rachel Haggard, who instilled fundamental values and an appreciation for genuine godliness in me. Without their influence this book would have been impossible. Thank you.

Contents

Section I: The Colorado Springs Model

Section II: Five Primary Principles

Section III: Lifestyle Warfare: Seven Power Points

Section IV: Our Responsibility to Primary Purpose

Charts

Illustrations

One of the most amazing phenomena that has occurred during my lifetime and my Christian ministry has been the distinct geographical shift in the center of gravity of American evangelicalism.

When I first became aware of such things, the New York-Philadelphia axis was the prestige center. New York City held the Sudan Interior Mission, Calvary Baptist Church, the headquarters of the Christian and Missionary Alliance and their huge tabernacle, and many other ministries. In Philadelphia one could find the China Inland Mission, Westminster Seminary, the *Sunday School Times* and Donald Gray Barnhouse's Tenth Presbyterian

Church and his *Eternity Magazine.*

After World War II, the center of gravity began to shift to Wheaton, Illinois. Anchored by Wheaton College and near to Moody Church in Chicago, Wheaton became a magnet for evangelical mission organizations and publishers and other ministries. The National Association of Evangelicals made Wheaton its headquarters. The city became fondly known as "The Evangelical Vatican."

During the 1970s and 1980s Pasadena, California, and Tulsa, Oklahoma, showed signs of becoming new centers of gravity, but neither was to become a successor to Wheaton. It was only as we entered the 1990s that a new geographical nerve center destined to lead American evangelicalism into the twenty-first century became evident: Colorado Springs, Colorado.

Previous to that, Colorado Springs was not at all unknown. Two significant ministries had anchored themselves there: The Navigators and Young Life. But the general public saw Colorado Springs more as a center of New Age and the occult rather than a center of evangelical Christianity. Among some, the city had gained the reputation for being a graveyard for pastors. This began to change radically when Pastor Ted Haggard moved to Colorado Springs in 1985.

Ten years later it now would be difficult to find a well-informed Christian leader in the U.S.A. who is unaware that Colorado Springs has become the "Wheaton of the West." At this writing more than eighty Christian ministries have relocated their headquarters to Colorado Springs. Among the largest are the Christian and Missionary Alliance from the New York area, David C. Cook Publishing from the Wheaton area, and Focus on the Family from the Pasadena area. The social, political, economic, moral and spiritual climate of the city is radically different from only five years ago. A surprising article in a recent issue of the *Washington*

14

Post with the title, "In Colorado Springs Religious Groups Have the Right of Way," says, "If you flipped the Democrat-dominated District of Columbia on its head, you would get Colorado Springs." It goes on to highlight the tangible influence that Bible-believing Christians have had on the city.[1]

How did all this happen?

Many others have their stories yet to tell, but we now have an important part of the answer to this question from one of the major players, Pastor Ted Haggard of New Life Church. As you read this book, you will feel the heart of God Himself beating through Ted Haggard. He does not write to glorify himself or his church, but to glorify the Lord Jesus who sent him and his wife, Gayle, to Colorado Springs from Baker, Louisiana.

I will never forget the first time I entered the worship auditorium of New Life Church. At Fuller Seminary I function as professor of church growth in the School of World Mission. I see myself as a professional missiologist with a specialty in church growth. When I first saw the size of the New Life worship auditorium and its remarkable interior decoration, I knew at once I was in a local church that dramatically personified my own passions. Number one, the seating capacity was approximately four thousand. Number two, hanging from the ceiling were the flags of every nation in the world! While New Life Church was obviously making a powerful impact on its own community of Colorado Springs, it was plain to see that its vision did not end there. It is also one of the most thoroughly missions-minded churches I have yet seen.

I told Ted Haggard that if I ever moved to Colorado Springs I would want to join New Life Church!

Of the countless books I have in my library written by pastors of local churches, *Primary Purpose* is unique. There is much here about New Life Church, but there's no hint that "other churches should do it our way." Just the opposite. Ted Haggard highlights many other pastors and churches in Colorado Springs by name as models for ministry. Ted deeply believes in all the gifts of the Holy Spirit, but he consistently lifts the fruit of the Spirit higher than the gifts. He holds strong convictions on many issues, naming many of them explicitly, but always with humility and deep respect for those who may differ with him. He knows how to impart faith and optimism without being triumphalistic.

Many of us have been praying for some time that our cities would be visibly changed by the power of God. *Primary Purpose* will be a tremendous help for us in two ways: 1) it will build our faith to know for sure that it can be done, and 2) it will give us practical steps on the pathway to see a new spiritual climate come to our own communities.

C. Peter Wagner
Fuller Theological Seminary
Pasadena, California

Our bookshelves are full of Christian books and videos. We have churches on every major street, more staff people than ever before, large Sunday school departments, cell systems, mega- and meta-church seminars. We have Christian bumper stickers, political action groups, huge parachurch ministries and extensive social programs. We have built huge churches, ministries, universities and homes — and in the midst of it all, we have lost every major city in North America.

We have beautiful seminaries, wonderful libraries and scholarly theological analysis. People in some churches are laughing, resting in the spirit and vigorously interceding.

Other churches are tired, broke and bitter. Our own TV, radio and literature campaigns make us believe that we are making a difference. And our prophets tell us that we are — but the statistics don't.

It's time for a level-headed, Spirit-dominated, Bible-based return to our primary purpose. It can be done. This book provides four sections of proof.

- Section 1 demonstrates the facts.

- Section 2 reveals five proven principles that can be used anywhere to cause the body of Christ to be more effective.

- Section 3 stresses biblical virtues and teachings that are necessary to make the five principles work — I call them "lifestyle warfare."

- Section 4 is the charge: We are the ones equipped and responsible for making a difference. And changing our cities is not only possible, it is easy (and natural for us as Christians).

THE
COLORADO SPRINGS
MODEL

One

UNUSUAL
BEGINNINGS

The phone jarred me from a deep sleep. At first no one answered in response to my startled and groggy hello. I could hear music playing in the background and the faint sound of people talking.

Then a voice spoke menacingly into the phone. "We control this city, and we will control you. You've opened your stupid mouth too many times, so we will destroy you — and your family. We will stop you and those like you," the man went on. "We will bury you alive. We want you to suffer."

I sat up in bed. "Who is this?"

The caller ignored my question. "We are everywhere, and we will get you. If you stay in this town, you will suffer, Ted

Haggard — you and your family."

"I bind you, devil, in the name of Jesus!" I exclaimed. The caller had my full attention.

"All it takes is a trip to the mailbox, a moment alone in the yard or a walk with your dog. We will get you. You will not succeed. We know why you're here, and we will stop you. If you don't leave this town now, we'll make sure you'll wish you'd never come to Colorado Springs."

Click.

Our bedroom seemed dark and cold. My wife, Gayle, asked innocently, "Who was it, honey?"

I avoided giving her an answer. "I need a drink of water." Then I got up to check on our children. As I went from room to room, I thought, "What a welcome Colorado Springs has given us! Where did these people come from?"

Welcome to Colorado Springs

Colorado Springs, like other American cities, had gained a reputation of being a pastors' graveyard. Most newly planted churches failed. Pastors became discouraged because of attendance and financial problems. They had tried to promote unity and harmony, and prayer groups had formed throughout the city. But relationships were strained, and the body of Christ was fragmented.

"The last thing this city needs is more churches," a veteran pastor said at a weekly pastors' breakfast, looking at me I was the only one there about to start a new church. "You'll understand in ten or fifteen years, after you realize how flaky Colorado Springs Christians are and how much it will cost you to try to pastor in this city."

I sat in silence, a little embarrassed.

After the meeting some men stayed to drink coffee. "Have you heard about the cattle mutilations that go on around here?" one asked me. He reported that farmers find their cattle dead in the fields, with tongues, lips, hearts, ears and reproductive organs removed, apparently with a sharp knife. Some report no tire tracks or blood.

"We found fetishes in front of our door last Sunday," another pastor said, describing his troubling church situation.

"I think it's all satanists," another stated. "They fast and pray against us too. They hate us."

"A lady tried to escape the control of her coven a couple of years ago," one pastor began. "She told us how they trained their children in satanism. They would take them to coven meetings and make them participate in actual sacrifices and all that goes along with that. The children would personally experience demonic spiritual power.

"When these kids were in their early teens," the pastor continued, "their parents would take them to visit a powerless Christian church.

"'Did you experience any power at the Christian church?' the parents asked afterward. The teens would always answer an honest no. 'Then who do you believe is really alive, Satan or Jesus Christ?'

"The obvious answer was always Satan. Soon after that, the teens would be taken through a ritual that would confirm them as satanists."

It was hard for me to believe these things were happening in a city that appeared so normal. After all, the downtown churches, like First United Methodist, First Baptist and First Presbyterian, seemed stable and consistent. And some of the liberal and anticharismatic churches were prospering.

Only one charismatic church, Faith Christian Fellowship, had increased to 550 people, but this was short-lived. Most charismatic ministries had struggled, but Gayle and I had confidence in God's direction.

One afternoon I was praying for a dramatic outpouring of God's kingdom in Colorado Springs and the surrounding areas. I was suddenly struck by my own inadequacy

"Father, I don't know how to do this! I have never started a church before. Lord, You have to help Gayle and me."

Then, in the middle of my desperation, the Lord comforted me. "I am going to bless you to confound those who think they know what they are doing." That did it. I knew I didn't have to be an expert to succeed. God wanted to perform a miracle in this city.

Birthing a Church in Our Basement

In January 1985 we held our first service in the basement of our home on Lightning Way. I stacked three five-gallon buckets on top of one another to use as a pulpit and asked the believers who joined with us to bring their lawn chairs. The basement was unfinished, cold and bare.

Our worship leader had to hitchhike to some of the meetings, but he was faithful. One Sunday during a blizzard he caught a ride in the back of a pickup truck. Snow covered his head and shoulders and slowly melted while he played his guitar. It didn't matter to us; we were looking for hope and purpose, not a performance.

People came from all walks of life, from a successful accountant to a woman known in town as the "worm lady." To make money, she would go out and collect worms in the street medians at night when the water sprinklers were running, wearing a raincoat and a miner's hat. But we had a sense of excitement and destiny and believed we were special.

One time when I was praying about the lack of qualified people, I turned in my Bible to 1 Samuel 22:2. There I found a description of the people who were added to David when he was alone. "All those who were in distress or in debt or discontented gathered around him, and he became their leader."

That described our band of twenty-five. We probably had such a great time because of our innocence and inexperience. We barely knew each other, but we always felt a sense of expectancy as we gathered for worship, Bible study and prayer.

I knew I had to inform my neighbors about the meetings we were going to hold.

"You can use your home for four months to start the church," one neighbor said. Then he added, "Having a church in your home is a code violation, but we won't report you as long as you don't disturb the neighborhood."

I was determined to respect my neighbors and give them no cause for concern. My purpose was to be a blessing, not a curse. Since we were meeting in a residential area, I knew my neighbor was right. One complaint to the city would force us to stop meeting, so we implemented strict rules about parking and noise while emphasizing a servant's mentality.

1. No parking in front of anyone else's house.
2. Park in the field at the end of the street and walk quietly to our home.
3. No congregating or loud talking in groups outside
4 No walking on anyone else's property.
5 No littering
6. Don't attract unnecessary attention to yourself.

My neighbors were still concerned about people coming and going and about more traffic. I visited each one, assuring them we would not meet in the house after April and thanked them for their patience. They were glad I had communicated openly with them and said that the people had been very nice. But they underscored the four-month limit.

Spiritual Reactions

I didn't understand why at the time, but over the next four months our lives were crazy.

One day I was working in my garage. Jack Hall, a student

from Christ for the Nations Institute, was visiting us and playing in the yard with my children, Christy and Marcus.

A young woman I had known for a few weeks through the church approached our house.

"Hello, Pastor Ted. How are you?" the young woman said as she walked up the driveway. She seemed troubled.

"Fine, fine. It's good to see you today. What brings you all the way out here?" I asked.

As the young woman stepped closer, she reached down to her ankle, as if she wanted to scratch her leg. Instead she pulled a five-inch knife out of a leg sheath and lunged toward me. I grabbed her wrist and pulled the knife out of her hand as Jack raced over to help me.

"I'm sorry, Pastor Ted! Something is wrong with me, very wrong!" she cried. "I don't know why I am doing what I am doing. I feel completely out of control."

"Don't worry — you're going to be all right," I assured her. I prayed with her, then told her to go home. Jack took her to her car; she had hidden it on the other side of a neighbor's house.

I was starting to understand an unusual spiritual dynamic that was not the young woman's fault.

Another time, at a Wednesday night prayer meeting, everything seemed normal until one man stepped outside to get something from his car. He rushed back in to tell us a woman was in the field behind our house screeching like a cat.

We knew why she was there. We were praying for the city, and her coven made it her responsibility to try to negate the prayers. (Making cat-like screeching noises is a common practice of demonized people who attempt to call forth additional demons.) We were not alarmed or afraid, only embarrassed that our neighbors might have heard the loud screeching and wondered what we were doing. I never said a word to them about it.

Often Gayle and I woke up at night sensing that people

25

were approaching our home from the field behind our house. I would get up and turn on the outside lights. That was the closest feeling to terror that we experienced in the early days of the church. We would pray together and then try to go back to sleep.

Threatening telephone calls were a weekly occurrence, particularly on Saturday nights: "You'll be dead tomorrow. We're going to kill you. We'll shoot you in the morning in front of those fanatics. You'll never see your kids again."

Another threatened, "Any more impertinence out of you, Ted Haggard, and there will be unrelenting pandemonium in this city."

These calls were laced with filthy expletives I wouldn't even begin to describe in this book. Gayle or I began to unplug the phone on Saturday nights as our normal routine.

We wondered about the character of the people visiting our church and whether they were spies from the covens. Weird people were coming to our home, but we didn't know how they were finding us.

Unless it was through the spiritual world — because of the prayer meetings.

Prayer: Communion and Confrontation

Shortly after we started the church, I invited a handful of men to pray with me in my basement on a cold winter night. One man in the group — I'll call him Ron — said God was revealing to him that a demonic, religious spirit named Control was at work in our city. He said that the Holy Spirit actually enabled him to see the spirit. Ron sensed that Control was masquerading as a good spirit that had gained authority in several key churches in the area.

Now the spirit had come to assume authority over our newly birthed church.

We were not about to let that happen. I and the others commanded the evil spirit to bow "in the name of the Lord

Jesus Christ." At once I sensed resistance; the spirit was refusing to bow. Ron could "see" the spirit, like the silhouette of a man struggling with an unseen opponent.

We continued to pray. "We command you, in the name of the Lord Jesus Christ, to bow to His lordship. Because of the cross, because of the blood and because of the Word of God, you must submit to His lordship."

For forty minutes we battled in prayer. "In the name of the Lord Jesus Christ, we announce to you that you will never exercise any control over New Life Church and that you are now forbidden to make any other churches in this city controlling, manipulative or judgmental. You must bow. You have no choice. You are defeated. Now bow in the name of Jesus!"

In an instant we knew that what we had prayed for was accomplished. Ron saw Control fall to its knees. We felt invigorated, relieved and pleased that we had actually engaged and defeated an enemy. But we wondered if this little prayer meeting in the basement of my home might create more conflict with the religious demonic powers in the area.

Tangible Results

Even though weird things were happening, we decided not to talk about them in our Sunday believers' meetings or even make an issue of them in our Wednesday night prayer meetings. Instead we increased our commitment to pursue God's plan for our region and talked about His vision for Colorado Springs. We confronted the enemy aggressively in private while denying him unnecessary attention in public.

Our basement church grew in attendance from twenty-five believers to over seventy by the end of April. But we didn't appear to be doing anything right. According to the church growth books, our location, publicity, facilities, printing, parking, staff and finances were wrong — everything was wrong except our hearts.

So, just as the four months ended, the Lord faithfully provided a series of miracles that allowed us to move the church from the basement into a public location. In the midst of those miracles and the strange spiritual encounters, we prayed and fasted more. That helped us find the core reason to press on through the opposition and keep taking the risk that someone would even physically harm us. In short, the devil had pushed too far. People had threatened us too much. We articulated our primary purpose: to make it hard to go to hell from Colorado Springs.

God was planting His vision in us — His vision for our city and for Colorado.

On one prayer retreat, I saw in my heart a stadium with thousands of men praising God. Armies of men.[1]

On another occasion, I saw a center where people could go to pray and fast and meet exclusively with the Lord. No counselors. No therapists. Just open spaces, beautiful mountains and prayer.[2]

On a third occasion, I saw a world prayer center where people were coming from all over the world to pray for global evangelism. In the prayer center, intercessors could go into a sphere with a huge globe to pray for people around the world.[3]

Another vision was of New Life Church, full of people worshipping and praising God, learning the Scriptures in an atmosphere of freedom and security.

Then it dawned on me: God has a specific dream for my life, my family, my city and my state. We are to be ambassadors of His dream and co-laborers with Him to fulfill it.

Fresh Ideas Through Prayer and Fasting

As we grew into and out of larger and larger buildings, the Lord was teaching us about being a catalyst for God's vision in a city. Since none of us had ever participated in a church that thought aggressively of an entire city in these terms, we prayed and fasted regularly, asking God to give us ideas.

And as we prayed together, our prayers seemed to take a supernatural direction.

- We prayed that the resources of our city would be used for global evangelism.

- We prayed that Colorado Springs would become a place of refuge for Christians to raise their children and enjoy their homes in peace.

- We prayed for all the people in our region to be exposed to an understandable presentation of the gospel.

- We prayed that God would call our young men and women to participate in His global plan.

- We prayed that churches would combine solid, biblical understanding with a fresh flow in His Spirit.

During times of prayer and fasting, we realized that the harvest was prime in Colorado Springs. I sensed that at least twenty thousand people were prepared by God to come to Christ. They would not need to be persuaded. The Lord had already prepared them; we just needed to reach them.

Our faith was high.

Our responsibility was clear.

One time I rented a room at a local hotel to pray and fast. From my room I could see the northern portion of Colorado Springs. Worship music was playing in the background. I had been praying and meditating on the Scriptures when I started to feel as if my hands were dirty and something was on them. I kept wringing them to get whatever it was off. Suddenly I realized it was the blood of people's lives on my hands.

The Lord was apparently showing me that I did not have the privilege of just reading my Bible, praying nice prayers and pastoring a pleasant little church. I had to help rescue a lot of people from impending eternal disaster. I knew the responsibility was mine. I could not displace it on someone else or create excuses for failure. I knew God would hold me responsible.

So I begged for mercy and went to work.

A Grand Experiment

By now I feared God too much to focus exclusively on New Life Church. His dream for our city was much greater than one pastor or even one local church. Once we realized that New Life Church was to be a catalyst for a larger vision that would require the participation of many churches, our prayers and vision for outreach grew.

I became obsessed with the grand experiment of living in a city where every citizen is exposed to an understandable presentation of the gospel. Our theme was a slogan that I learned from Danny Ost, the great missionary to Mexico: Win the lost at any cost because people last forever.

To get into the secular world, we purchased thirty-second TV spots that promoted the Lord and the Bible on the most ungodly television programs, and we taped Christian testimonials to air on secular radio. We designed beautiful signs about Jesus for our city buses, billboards, taxi cabs and baseball stadiums.

I knew God's Spirit was giving us ideas that could effectively reach into our community. His desire to reach people seemed overwhelming. He wanted us to seize this city for Him. He wanted us to make it hard to go to hell from Colorado Springs. And He started adding people to our church who knew how to do it.

Two

THE SIEGE

Colorado Springs is full of unsung heroes. One of those is Bob Edwards. I remember when he introduced himself to me after a service. He was clean-cut, in his early twenties and mellow. I liked him immediately.

"Hi, my name's Bob," he said, while looking around the sanctuary. "Can we talk?"

"Sure, I'd love to. I'm glad you came this morning," I said.

When we met later he explained that he and some friends had been attending another church in town. Because of the unusual prayer meetings they held in the church, however, their church had asked them to leave.

"We've been axed," he told me and asked if they could

use our church for their prayer meetings. "Some friends and I feel as if God is showing us some of the demonic powers over this city that are keeping the churches from growing and keeping people from accepting Christ. That's what we are praying about. We're not flakes or anything like that. We just want to pray."

Bob and his friends had already been praying in the city for four years, but they felt as if pastors and church leaders had always kept them at a distance. I agreed with what he was saying, but spiritual warfare was not a popular subject at the time. That's why I didn't speak publicly about my own experiences. But spiritual warfare was vital to our purpose.

"Listen, brother," I said. "I'm for anything that builds the body of Christ. You can use our building for prayer meetings anytime you like as long as they promote the Lord."

Two weeks later Bob and a group of young men were in our sanctuary on a Friday night praying over a five-gallon metal bucket of cooking oil.

"We asked God what to do, and He told us to anoint the city with oil," Bob explained. "We've seen people go forward and get a drop of oil on their foreheads, so for the city we got a pump-up garden sprayer to take out with us when we pray. It holds five gallons, and I think it works."

All right, I thought, it's a little unusual. But so is Colorado Springs.

Step 1: Prayer

Bob and his friends waged guerilla warfare on a spiritual level. They worshipped, prayed in the Spirit, confronted evil forces and prayed for angels to overpower the darkness. It was like a Frank Peretti book come to life — and that was only the prayer meetings.

Then they traveled throughout the city anointing major intersections, spiritual power points and churches. They sprayed oil on the pavement and the grass but showed respect to property owners by not putting it on buildings or windows. Bob and his friends visited fifteen houses that were said to be owned by witches and prayed over them. Within a month, ten of those fifteen houses went up for sale.

People involved with demonic powers claimed to be persecuted in Colorado Springs. When asked how they were being persecuted, they could never give a tangible answer. They just knew there was something wrong with their ability to appropriate evil spiritual power. As a result, they either got saved or moved to what they considered a more "friendly spiritual climate."

"Do you know how long oil stays on pavement?" Bob asked me one time. "It's there forever."

And that's exactly the kind of impact this city needs, I thought.

Not only were Bob Edwards and others praying against demonic powers, but our church was praying for the Holy Spirit to bless every person in Colorado Springs — literally. We cut up the pages of the phone book into little pieces with five names on each piece. Every church member received five names to pray for each week.

After praying for the people listed in the phone book, we asked God to prosper and bless the businesses. The churches in the yellow pages received special attention. We wanted God to cause every church in our city to become a growing, life-giving church.*

But that wasn't enough. We asked people to visit schools and shopping centers — any place people gathered — and pray discreetly for them. We have prayed especially for government workers, asking God to give them ideas to bless our city and make it a better place to live. When our police department and other government agencies initiate pro-

* A life-giving church is one that emphasizes the absolutes of Scripture and imparts the life of Christ. In some cities the life-giving churches might be charismatic and Presbyterian, while in other cities they may be Baptist and Assemblies of God. I believe that 50 percent of the churches in Colorado Springs are life-giving.

grams that work, we rejoice with them in their success.

We also encouraged people to get a map of the city and pray over it neighborhood by neighborhood. Don Lovell, a member of the congregation, organized systematic prayer walks throughout the entire city. (Prayer walking simply means that you go to the actual place where you want to see an answer to prayer and pray on location. If you want to pray for the business center of a city, you go there and walk through the area praying discreetly. You don't need to draw any attention to yourself.)

"When you see a 'For Sale' sign," I told people who were prayer walking, "that is your opportunity — right there." Those properties were in transition. We wanted them to be purchased in accordance with God's will. I believe that praying for God to be glorified through properties that were for sale or being developed played a major role in cultivating the spiritual life of our city.

I've prayed for hundreds of such properties. One time Tim Ost (the son of missionary Danny Ost) and I prayed over two large buildings that had been built for high-tech manufacturing. Millions of dollars had been invested in the construction of those buildings. We walked around the property praying for the Lord to "take it off the open market in Jesus' name," asking that only the Holy Spirit would give permission for someone to buy it.

As we were anointing the doors with oil, we must have set off an alarm because we suddenly heard police sirens heading in our direction.

I'm embarrassed to say that we got so flustered that we hid in a field of grass just before the police cars pulled up. (The right thing to do would have been simply to apologize and explain what we were doing.) The officers looked all around the building and finally left. Then we crawled out of the grass and went home too.

Even though we made a few mistakes, I believe God honored the spirit of our prayers. Those buildings didn't sell for five years until David C. Cook, a Christian publishing company, bought the property. They tore down the largest of the two buildings and are currently building a new structure so they can spread the gospel through printed material. For the sake of the previous owners of the buildings, I only wish that we had prayed for a *quick* sale.

We bathed the city in prayer. But prayer wasn't an end in itself. It was to prepare people for evangelism. It was an essential part of our primary purpose — to make it hard to go to hell from Colorado Springs. Without prayer, evangelism wouldn't work.

Step 2: United Evangelism Supported by Prayer

A friend named Tom Perkins, who runs an auto dealership with his father, came to me with an idea one summer. "For the past few years, my father and I have been making thirty-second TV spots to air during the Christmas season to encourage people to come to Christ. We would like to give the New Life Church phone number during the spots and have people call here for prayer."

"That's exactly why we're here," I said. "If you take care of the ads, then we'll set up phone counselors and help get people saved. We'll also organize a prayer team."

The first year we were involved, we had seven phone lines. Six churches sent people to answer phones and follow up on new believers.

The second year we had twelve lines. Fourteen churches helped.

The third year we had twenty-one lines with forty-five churches helping lead people to Christ.

We received an overwhelming response after each spot was aired. The lines lit up one after the other until every counselor was busy. Then Methodists, Nazarenes, Presbyterians, Baptists, Lutherans, Pentecostals and people from the Navigators and Compassion International all sat side-by-side, leading people to the Lord.

The spiritual hunger was so great in our city that one night, after the phone lines were closed, we received a fax in huge handwritten letters saying, "Open your lines. I need spiritual help NOW!"

We were united around our primary purpose. We didn't ask for money; we didn't promote any particular local church. We just told them about Jesus. We obtained their addresses so we could send them literature that repeated information about coming to Christ and encouraged them to become involved with one of the life-giving churches in town.

Then another local businessman, Gene Bath, volunteered to produce and pay for thirty-second spots on radio that promoted the gospel and gave out our same phone number. That made the lines light up between the television spots, too.

The television spots aired over a seven-day period from 5:30 to midnight every evening on several different television stations. About 175 spots were broadcast over the course of the week.

In 1986, for example, 4,932 people called. Approximately 700 of them made first-time commitments to Jesus.

The television ads were a great idea. But I also know beyond a shadow of a doubt that we only had success because we paved the way with prayer. That truth was driven home for me when we participated in the *JESUS* Film Project in Colorado Springs.

Campus Crusade for Christ asked the Colorado Springs churches to distribute the *JESUS* video door-to-door throughout the city. They told us to expect 30 percent of the homes to take a video; for every two videos we distributed, there would be one first-time conversion. They projected those figures from previous *JESUS* video campaigns.

New Life Church agreed to distribute the tape in thirty of three hundred precincts in Colorado Springs. During the week before we gave away videotapes, we walked through the neighborhoods hanging a flyer about the video on the front door of each home. But the primary purpose of the flyer was not the flyer. It was to touch every door and pray that the video would be received when we started the campaign. I did some teaching on prayer walking; then we prayed over the cases of videos and trusted God to prepare the hearts of the people to receive the tapes as we went from door to door.

Later, volunteers visited each house with an armload of tapes and said, "Hi. We're distributing *JESUS* videos. This is a video about the life of Christ. If you want it, there are no strings attached. We will give it to you free of charge if you'll just promise to watch it."

Seventy percent of the homes in each precinct accepted the tape — compared to the national average of 30 percent. In some precincts 90 percent of the homes took the tape!

I had to stand up on a Sunday morning and say, "We're in trouble. God is answering our prayers. We need to take a special offering to buy thousands of additional tapes!" That Sunday the people gave enough to buy tapes for all who wanted one.

Step 3: Healthy Attitudes Prevail in the Midst of Evangelism

We learned that, with adequate prayer, evangelistic efforts become very effective. "Colorado Springs is the easiest city I know of in which to lead people to Christ," I told others. Then we observed a supernatural by-product — that in the midst of prayer and evangelism believers automatically focus on their primary purpose. Prayer provides life, spiritual illumination and focus upon purpose. Because of prayer, then, evangelistic efforts are increasingly effective, which is encouraging to the body. As a result, mutual respect in the body of Christ has an opportunity to increase.

In this environment,

- Evangelicals don't preach against charismatics.
- Charismatics are respectful of evangelicals.
- Bible-believing liberals are open to the conservative evangelicals and the charismatics.
- Leaders of the larger churches genuinely enjoy one another.
- Strained relationships heal, and long-term friendships develop.

When we understood that together we could do powerful things that would have been impossible alone, the percentage of people attending life-giving churches increased. This church growth was not confined to any one particular group or tradition within the Christian community. Instead the deciding factor was whether or not the church was promoting the life that is in Christ.

We sent a survey to some of the pastors of the life-giving churches in our city to try to measure the growth rate. These groups included conservative Baptists, Presbyterians, independent charismatics, Assemblies of God, Nazarenes and others. They reported that their average growth from 1985 to 1993 exceeded 8.5 percent per year. Our own church was growing at a rate of ten families a week. Each week for a period of four years we led up to fifty people in prayer as they made first-time commitments to Christ.

In this environment, then, it was not difficult for believers to be respectful and supportive in their speech and actions toward one another.

- Several charismatic pastors stopped meeting exclusively together so that they could meet regularly with the evangelical pastors.

- One local church sent baby-sitters free of charge to help another local church of a different denomination

- When the Ku Klux Klan planned a rally in Colorado Springs, over two hundred churches presented a specially prepared Sunday school series that showed the biblical support for the equality of all human beings. Christians united in prayer, asking God to keep the KKK rally from being an issue in our city. No one came to the rally. The city yawned.

Step 4: Natural By-Product — Societal Change

To evaluate the effectiveness of our efforts in prayer, evangelism and church growth, we looked at secular society to see if we were making an impact. We needed to know if people outside our own groups were being affected. After all, what benefit was it if we were doing wonderful "Christian" activities that impressed us but were of no concern to the secular community and generated no interest in the gospel? We came to the conclusion that:

1. If our prayers were really effective, life-giving churches would grow because of the increase in conversions.

2. If genuine conversion growth were taking place in a broad way in our city, it would result in a measurable societal shift.

These societal indicators differ from city to city. But we must evaluate our effectiveness by indicators in our society at large rather than indicators that are exclusively within our own churches (2 Cor. 10:12). For us, we recognized a societal shift when we experienced:

1. More parachurch ministries moving to our city

2. Declining crime rates
3. Dramatically reduced satanic coven activity

1. More Parachurch Ministries Moving to Our City

As believers were praying and working together, our city economic development commission solicited parachurch ministries to move to Colorado Springs. Parachurch ministries are broad-based organizations that operate beyond a local level. After the leaders at these ministries prayed and felt the Lord leading them to Colorado Springs, they were also encouraged to come because of the healthy relationships among the churches and the positive attitudes of the believers.

From 1989 to 1994 the number of Christian parachurch ministries tripled in the city. The *Washington Post* put the number at fifty-four, describing the impact as roughly equivalent to what the "lobbying trade is to Washington."[1] The number of Christian radio stations increased from two to six. Ministries such as James Dobson's Focus on the Family, Overseas Crusade, AD 2000 and Beyond, and Every Home for Christ joined with ministries already in the Colorado Springs region. These included the International Bible Society, the world headquarters for the Christian and Missionary Alliance, Young Life, the Navigators and Compassion International.

These, along with dozens of smaller ministries, started to transform Colorado Springs from being just a conservative city to becoming "The Vatican of Evangelical Christianity" and "The Wheaton of the West." These ministries believed in the Bible as the Word of God and in the ministry of the Holy Spirit.

Just like the local churches, some of them, such as Compassion International, Focus on the Family and the International Bible Society, grew phenomenally from 1989 to 1994. Even among ministries that did not grow dramatically, there was a sense of optimism because of what was happening in the community.

The increasing number of parachurch ministries in town-was positive for the local churches, too. Colorado Springs now has one of the most active chapters of the Christian Management Association and a very active chapter of the National Association of Evangelicals. The influence of para-church organizations has forced those of us in local church-es to maintain a broad perspective of ministry and keep our primary purpose before us.

Our city was changing in a measurable way.

2. Declining Crime Rates

For two major reasons crime rates are good indicators of societal change. First, Christians should not be involved in criminal activity because Scripture commands us to honor those in authority (Rom. 13:1-3). If Christians increase in an area, crime should decrease because fewer people are likely to commit it.

Second, in the spiritual realm, demons constantly tempt people to sin, including taking part in criminal activity. Some crimes are committed by people who are controlled by evil spirits. When Christians pray for all the people of a city, their prayers inhibit the influence of evil spirits toward crime.

Chart 1 on the next page shows the change in the Colorado Springs crime rate from 1980 to 1993.

Before 1985 the crime rates both rose and fell. But after people became organized in systematic prayer for the city in 1985 and 1986, the crime rate dropped consistently for seven years.

Even though there are exceptions to this trend (for example, other statistics show the number of murders has risen slightly over the years as our population has grown), the positive contributions to the atmosphere of the city are noticeable.

In 1994 police spokesman Rich Resling told the Colorado Springs *Gazette Telegraph* that crime in the city had

Chart 1

Index Crime Rates 1980 – 1993[*]
Colorado Springs, CO

Year	Number of Crimes	Popu- lation[†]	Index Crime Rate[‡]
1980	16,910	214,821	79
1981	18,837	226,230	83
1982	18,453	229,770	80
1983	18,096	236,760	76
1984	17,918	241,270	74
1985	21,835	253,300	86
1986	22,833	265,700	86
1987	22,826	269,500	85
1988	22,174	273,000	81
1989	21,553	275,500	78
1990	21,017	281,140	75
1991	21,444	285,350	75
1992	20,194	290,977	69
1993	19,609	299,343	66

* The index crime rate is a key indicator of the level of crime in a city. Index crimes are murder, rape, robbery, aggravated assault, burglary, larceny and motor vehicle theft. (Negligent manslaughter is not included in the FBI's crime index.) Index crime data came from the Colorado Springs Police Department's annual statistical reports for 1980 – 1993.

† Population data came from the Colorado Springs planning, development and finance office.

‡ The index crime rate is the number of index crimes per one thousand people in the population.

declined to a level that makes it among the safest cities of its size in the nation.[2]

I know Christians can't take all the credit for the change because many other positive influences have contributed to it. But I don't think the change could have taken place *without* prayer, evangelism and new converts.

3. *Declining Satanic Activity*

During this same time period, our prayer teams were reporting a major decline in satanic activity. We tracked this through reports from new converts who had been involved in the occult. During the early days of the church, new converts would describe a prospering occult community with thousands of participants. But by the nineties, people were telling us how the number of covens had dwindled to five at the most and that there were very few people left in them.

In addition, I was hearing about fewer and fewer cattle mutilations. Previously, reports had been astonishly common. From 1971 to 1985, there were over ten thousand reports of mutilations in Colorado and eight other Western states.[3] When I met with other pastors, I was also hearing far fewer discussions about churches being defaced with satanic graffiti or pastors getting hostile phone calls.

New Battle Lines

In churches throughout the city, families were being restored, dramatic deliverances were taking place, and hundreds were coming to Christ. People who were unemployed or underemployed were finding new and better opportunities. Many couples were experiencing renewal in their relationships with each other.

Our city's economic development council continued to encourage Christian ministries to move to town because they could see the positive effects. All seemed to go well, until....

Three

STAYING STEADY

Homosexual rights became the hottest issue in Colorado Springs in the fall of 1990. That's when the human relations commission for the city proposed adding sexual orientation to the list of criteria that people could use for an illegal discrimination suit.

The community's response was quick and visible. Hundreds of Christians, along with other people, appeared at the city council meetings to express their belief that individuals should not qualify for special protection under the law just because of their sexual activities. Because of public outcry, the city council turned down the recommendation by the human relations commission in early 1991.

Amendment 2

Many people were pleased with the city council's decision, but some wondered if the issue of sexual orientation would surface again. That's when a group of Christians from Colorado Springs formed Colorado for Family Values. They described themselves as a political group that challenged promotion of homosexuality through government agencies and schools.

Colorado for Family Values wrote what became known as Amendment 2 of the Colorado constitution. It prohibited claims of discrimination based on sexual orientation.

Funding against the amendment came from across the country. Ministerial groups spoke out against it, and a liberal church, which condones homosexual marriages, ran advertisements that reminded people of the holocaust and encouraged them to vote no on Amendment 2. Most major newspapers were against it, and the television markets in Denver and Boulder would not even allow pro-Amendment 2 advertisements on their stations. The Denver/Boulder region, which includes 70 percent of the state's population, was strongly opposed to it.

. In short, neither liberals nor conservatives expected Amendment 2 to pass. But it did.

- Supporting the amendment were 53.4 percent of the voters.

- Forty-eight counties approved it, with only fifteen counties rejecting it.

- Thirteen counties passed it with an even greater percentage of the vote than El Paso County (where Colorado Springs is located).

- El Paso County passed it with 65 percent of the vote.[1]

These results surprised both sides, but they reflected

broad-based support for the amendment. The county that supported it with the highest percentage of the vote was Kiowa County, which is predominantly Anglo, Hispanic and Native American farmers. Such strong support coming from the broad-based citizenry was never expected by the opponents of Amendment 2.

I am sure those who wanted to discredit the amendment realized it would never be overturned if farmers, innocent-looking mountain townspeople and average citizens were the ones blamed for it. They needed a villain, and that villain was created—the "manipulative," "well-financed," "well-organized," "deceitful" religious right of Colorado Springs.

The political angle was clear: They claimed the Christians in Colorado Springs were creating hatred and division in the state. A spokesperson for People for the American Way told an NBC evening news reporter: "The evangelical groups in Colorado Springs are working to deny innocent citizens their civil rights. They are hateful bigots that won't be satisfied until their political goals are achieved."

But the reporter had a difficult time finding evidence portraying the Christians as hateful. After showing the quote he cut away to a packed altar at New Life Church and said, "We have not found this to be true. Instead, the evangelicals of Colorado Springs seem perfectly contented bringing converts to Christ." Then the report showed me leading a large portion of the sinner's prayer.

But to the liberal political strategists, facts seemed to be irrelevant. "After all," they implied, "nice people would not have voted for Amendment 2 if conservative, radical churches like New Life Church and ministries like Focus on the Family had not taken advantage of them." Even our governor marched with hundreds of people in Denver protesting what they perceived as the darkness that was coming out of Colorado Springs.

Political Response to Societal Change

During the Amendment 2 controversy, I was getting calls from many of the major news organizations: *Los Angeles Times*, "ABC Evening News," Bill Moyers, *Time, New York Times, Chicago Tribune*, "NBC Nightly News," British Broadcasting Corporation, *The Denver Post*, International News Network, *Washington Post* and National Public Radio.

A reporter for the British Broadcasting Corporation met with me in my office.

"Where does your political action organization meet?" he asked.

I told him that we didn't have any political organizations in our church.

He looked perplexed and disappointed but asked again, "Who organizes the church's political involvement?"

I told him that no one did because New Life Church didn't have any political involvement.

Then he got to the point. "What is the church's position on Amendment 2?"

I told him the church was a-political and that it didn't have any view. "I am confident that some of the people within our church are for it and others are against it," I said.

Next he tried a new angle. "Reverend Haggard," he said, "what is the Bible's position on homosexuality?"

I answered his question — knowing that he would probably frame my explanation of the Bible's position into the church's political position — but I just kept talking about God's great plan for our lives and how He has a plan for all of us, even though we all miss His best for us from time to time — and he used it! Even though the world was very concerned about Christians in politics, their attention was giving us an opportunity to explain the gospel gently.

47

The whole political controversy came as a surprise. Nowhere in my reading on revival did it warn about a political reaction to growth in the body of Christ. But when you think about it, large numbers of people having positive encounters with the Lord will impact the way those people involve themselves in their communities.

For example, often we see people with difficult situations in their lives find the Lord, and their lives change. That change of heart also produces a change in the way they relate to their families, their jobs and their government.

I often get enthusiastic letters like this one.

Dear Pastor Ted,

I have to tell you what has happened to me in this past year since I found the Lord at New Life.

Before I knew Christ, my life was completely out of control. My wife resented me, my children were afraid of me, and I despised myself. I don't want to tell you the horrible things I used to do because I'm so different now. Back then I couldn't keep a job, maintain my home or even be concerned about what other people thought.

But because of Jesus my life has changed. I am involved in the school my kids go to, I have had the same job now for nine months, and I enjoy spending my extra time with my family at home and at church. Thank God for the new me.

Bill

Even though I had no intentions of changing the way Bill related politically toward the government, the encounter that he had at New Life probably affected his level of political involvement. For example, his renewed interest in his children and their lives could have lead him to speak to the school board about curriculum. In addition, as a wage earner, chances are he would also be more interested in how his government was spending and taxing the money he made.

I believe that hundreds of people like Bill are what influenced the spiritual climate in Colorado Springs. Because of our emphasis on our primary purpose, we experienced a natural change in the political landscape.

For a short time it seemed like the Christian community would be exonerated, but then the process of vilifying Christians intensified.

Celebrate Diversity

Major news networks and publications began showing pictures and videos of large crowds attending services at New Life and other churches to demonstrate that we had enough influence to deny others their civil liberties. Even though neither I nor New Life Church had participated in the Amendment 2 debate, the media didn't hesitate to use our size as an illustration of the "political" power of the religious community.

Even purely spiritual meetings lost their purity in the eyes of some in the community. Efforts to communicate the gospel and encourage people in the Lord were attached to a particular political position. It became difficult to communicate the gospel. Church was not just church. It was the religious right or left in the average citizen's mind.

Because people in our city became so sensitive to what Christians were doing, incidents that would have been routinely handled before Amendment 2 became the subject of community-wide discussion and analysis.

- A policeman was publicly reprimanded for handing a woman a tract while on duty.

- A mother who sent her child to church through a bus

ministry sued the church because she was not notified before her child was baptized.

- A civil-rights group, Citizens Project, was formed to monitor the activities of evangelicals in public arenas.

- A schoolteacher was demoted, disciplined and reassigned for showing a film depicting an abortion to her eighth-grade sex education class. She had showed the film in her classes the previous four years.[2]

- The El Pomar Foundation, an organization that worked to encourage economic growth in Colorado Springs, announced that for political reasons they would not give additional grants to Christian groups. They had previously given $4 million to Focus on the Family to help them move to Colorado Springs.

- Colorado Springs was identified as "ground zero" by several homosexual rights groups because of the strong Christian influence. They equated Christianity with a particular political position. As a result, a watchdog group named Ground Zero formed in Colorado Springs and started publishing *The Ground Zero News*.

- Christians wanting to volunteer in their children's public schools were looked at with suspicion and sometimes ridiculed.

- If citizens running for public office identified themselves as Christian or even attended a Bible-based church, they were branded as stealth candidates of the religious right.

- The economic development council stopped encouraging Christian ministries to move to Colorado Springs.

As a result, the very spiritual renewal God had so graciously given our city had been manipulated into an anti-Christian political tool

Again we encountered the strongman over Colorado Springs trying to intimidate and control the body of Christ, but this time he didn't confront us directly through demonic attack. Instead he worked to vilify the meaning of church, Christian, gospel and other related ideas. But his new tactic also failed.

Churches and parachurch ministries continued to grow

Christian groups continued to move to Colorado Springs.

Prayer teams continued to walk the streets, and new churches kept springing up, while older life-giving ones continued to grow.

How?

We kept our attention on our primary purpose

We acknowledged that political situations were important, but temporary. But our primary purpose wasn't just important; it was eternal.

I believe that, as responsible citizens, Christians should be involved in political issues. Even though we will be divided on most issues, there will be times when we will stand together. Some battles we will win; others we will lose. But the battle that must not be lost is the eternal struggle to liberate individuals spiritually, which will result in inspiring the whole community. In the midst of any political situation we must stay steady and keep our focus on our primary purpose: making it hard to go to hell from our cities.

Five years after the issue of homosexual rights became so prominent in Colorado Springs, the city is still known for having a strong Christian influence.[3] Though the watchdog groups are still active, the community attitude toward Christians is returning to what it was before the issue arose. We have learned that if we as Christians will be respectful and open toward all people and at the same time focus on our primary purpose, the gospel message can be communicated without other issues getting in the way.

I think churches and the Christian community rode through the storm because we recognized that our purpose for being in Colorado Springs was not political. It was spiritual.

And because spiritual purposes are so important, we were forced to discover an unusual combination of principles and lifestyles that continue to facilitate the advancement of the gospel in our city. To my knowledge, these principles were first articulated when I was asked to speak to some Christian leaders at a retreat for our local Association of Evangelicals.

THE FIVE
PRIMARY PRINCIPLES

Four

FOCUS ON
THE ABSOLUTES OF SCRIPTURE

(The first of five principles)

I was on my way to the meeting before I even had a chance to prepare what I was going to say. My friend Jim Tomberlin, pastor of Woodman Valley Chapel, asked me to speak at our local Association of Evangelicals' retreat for some Christian leaders of Colorado Springs. He wanted me to give the new ones an overview of the last few years.

As I thought about what to say to them, some wonderful people came to mind.

I thought of R. G. Dunbar, who had been praying for revival in Colorado Springs for thirty years, and of the many Women's Aglow home groups and the Navigator Bible study groups that were also praying. I thought of Richard Douglas and Don Steiger, who had invested their influence in building healthy relationships, and Bernie Kuiper and Billy Long who had stood firm for the cause of Christ in the midst of adversity. Then there were women like Pat Lichty and Julia Ramirez who had prayed and served the body of Christ for years. Dozens — if not hundreds — of individuals had been praying for God to do a miracle in Colorado Springs, and now that miracle had come.

As I drove to the retreat, I thought about specific principles we had all believed and practiced that were producing change in our city.

The first thought that came to my mind was that we focused on the absolutes of the Scripture. We stopped looking at the ways we were different and started to function in the ways we were alike.

Second, I thought, both the leaders and individual Christians in town determined to promote Christ and His Word above their particular church or way of doing things. That was a result of focusing on the absolutes.

Some people just yearned for the kingdom of God to grow in our city. They supported anybody who encouraged the gospel. I could picture a graph that showed the activity of the Holy Spirit in the city rising higher and higher because of their prayers. So I wrote down a third principle: Pray to raise the water level of the Holy Spirit's activity in the whole city.

I arrived at the retreat center and was about to get out of my car when I was struck by the scene in front of me. Pastors and parachurch leaders of all varieties were standing in small groups laughing and talking. Some groups were walking along the dirt roads joking, greeting newcomers with hugs and smiles, and directing one another to the proper buildings.

How can these guys do this? I thought. They worship differently, attend different churches and have totally different understandings of the Scriptures.

Then I wrote down the fourth principle: Appreciate one another's respected interpretations of Scripture. I called them "respected interpretations" because heresy would not be tolerated, but other "respected interpretations" were fine — even welcomed. I knew that these men recognized that some fine believers embraced various interpretations that others rejected.

When I finally got out of the car and went to register, I heard a man introducing a colleague to one of the new pastors in town.

"I'd like you to meet Steve Todd," he said. "He has a great heart to pray for the success of other pastors. You'll really enjoy knowing him. He's a blessing."

I sat down and noted principle five: Practice supportive speech and actions toward one another.

I've been talking about the five principles ever since. They are simple. They are practical. And they are proven.

What's at the Core?

Christians embrace the same core absolutes. We all agree that Jesus of Nazareth is the Messiah and that He came in the flesh to destroy the works of the devil (1 John 3:8). We know that through Him we have access to the Father and, therefore, eternal life (Eph. 2:18). In addition, we all believe the Bible is the primary source of information about God, and it is the standard we use to judge spiritual experiences and teaching (2 Tim. 3:16).

In other words, we believe Jesus Christ is the truth. He is the fact all mankind must face. We also believe the Bible is the written expression of the absolutes.

Absolutes are not subject to personal convictions, cultural trends or even feelings. They are the same at any time in any society. People commit their lives to Jesus today the same way they did thousands of years ago: come to Him in humble submission, turn from the world and confess His lordship. That's why principle No. 1 is to focus on the absolutes of Scripture. When we focus on absolutes, we are in agreement.

Look at the illustration on the next page. Everything we Christians believe fits somewhere in one of the four areas described.

At the center are the absolutes, the unchanging foundations of faith.

The next circle is interpretations. An interpretation is an explanation and application of the Scripture. We usually are interpreting when we read a passage of Scripture and then say, "Now this is what it means."

Then there are deductions. Deductions come from looking at several passages of Scripture and drawing conclusions.

Finally, there are subjective opinions, which are personal preferences, such as how long a church service should be or what styles of songs we should sing. Sometimes these opinions get ridiculous. For example, I know of a church in Mississippi that split over whether to put a hat rack in the lobby. During a business meeting at a church in Indiana, a pastor's wife slapped a deacon's wife while they were debating over the need for gutters on the outside of the building.

We all agree on the absolutes, but the interpretations, deductions and subjective opinions divide us. Certainly we will have the interpretations, deductions and subjective opinions. But we make a grave mistake when we don't separate them according to their importance.

For example, all biblical Christians believe in the importance of the Holy Spirit; but some prefer speaking about the "baptism in the Holy Spirit," while others prefer being "filled with the Holy Spirit." Some like "being controlled by the Holy Spirit," while others discuss "fellowship with the Holy

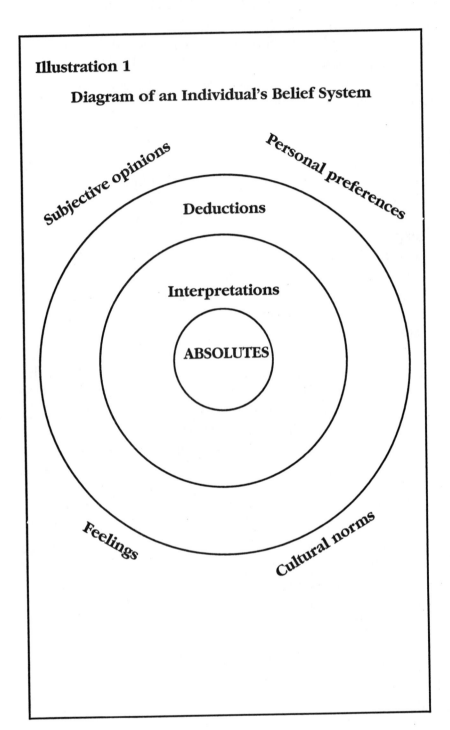

Illustration 1

Diagram of an Individual's Belief System

Subjective opinions

Personal preferences

Deductions

Interpretations

ABSOLUTES

Feelings

Cultural norms

Spirit." All realize the absolute necessity of the Holy Spirit's ministry; but because of various interpretations, deductions and subjective opinions about the Scripture verses that refer to the Holy Spirit, we have a differing emphasis on His ministry.

Believing the same absolutes, we differ on interpretation. That's why we have Christians who believe there is no biblical basis for the operation of such gifts as tongues or words of knowledge in this generation (cessationists). We also have Christians who believe all the gifts have the potential for full expression in the church today just as they did in the early church (Pentecostals, charismatics).

Absolutes Confused With Other Beliefs

I once heard a pastor teach about how Christians would be taken up in a silent rapture and enjoy the marriage supper of the Lamb for seven years while those left on earth would go through horrible persecution. Then, at the end of the seven years, Jesus and the raptured Christians would appear in the eastern sky, victoriously returning to begin the millennium. What amazed me was how he ended his sermon. He said, "If it doesn't happen this way, then Jesus Christ is not Lord."

This brother was equating deductions with an absolute.

The events of Christ's return may happen just as those who embrace pretribulation rapture theology predict. But whether or not the events occur in that precise fashion, Jesus is still Lord.

Most end-times theology is a deduction.

The lordship of Jesus Christ is an absolute.

But since this brother wasn't making this distinction in his own mind, then those who regularly received teaching from him probably would not make the contrast in their own thinking either. And without this clarification being made, this pastor and his students may reasonably conclude that if some people don't believe in pretribulation eschatology, then they are not biblical Christians. That would be a horrible mistake because they would become unable to identify the body of Christ in their own community and around the world. If we Christians can't even identify each other, it becomes very difficult to know if we are expanding God's kingdom effectively or not.

So we must not confuse what the Bible actually says with what we think it means because our culture and our subjective opinions influence our thinking processes.

While in Moscow two years ago I met some Christians who believed that it was an ungodly, sinful act to wear a tie. They believed it so strongly that they didn't think any genuine Christian could ever wear a tie because it pointed toward hell. I thought that was ridiculous and purely cultural and was proud that we in the West were so much more rational, until I heard a pastor talking about how significant his new church steeple was "because it pointed to heaven." His logic was identical to that of the brothers in Moscow! Both valued their purely cultural position.

We are destroying our potential for impact on a city's spiritual climate by highlighting our differences on nonessential issues. They unnecessarily divide us. We preach so vigorously on interpretations, but we sometimes fail to understand that our greatest strength is in the absolutes. When we believers start comparing ourselves to others on the basis of interpretations rather than absolutes, our influence is weakened.

Even though our nonessentials do have importance, they must never become the source of our identity. Our identity as Christians must be consciously based on the absolute core of our faith: Jesus Christ and His Word, the Bible.

If anyone equates interpretations with absolutes, that person will soon have a crisis of faith when one of his interpretations is challenged or proven false.

I recently met with a young couple who had a friend who told them the only way to be saved was through the King James translation (KJV) of the Bible. They were alarmed because our church uses the New International Version (NIV), which they had been told was not really a Bible at all.

I drew the three circles on a board for them, and we placed their items of concern in appropriate circles. When they saw that salvation issues were in the absolutes circle and their friend's opinions about the KJV fell in the area of subjective opinions and cultural norms, they understood. Their fears were relieved. Obviously, their friend was making a horrible mistake by equating absolutes with a cultural preference.

Do Dogs Go to Heaven?

When I was in high school, my little sister, Mary Lois, had a pet dog that died. I received the assignment of digging the grave and conducting a family service for the dog.

After a beautiful funeral, through her tears my cute little sister asked me if she would see her dog in heaven. I answered by explaining that dogs do not go to heaven because they don't have spirits and, therefore, can't receive eternal life as we human beings do. So, I concluded for her, her dog was gone — dust — never to be seen again.

She broke into deep sobs and ran into the house. Subsequently, my dad gave me the only spanking I received during my teen years. While in pain, the revelation struck me that no one knew with absolute certainty whether or not dogs go to heaven. Maybe those questions shouldn't be answered in the same way as questions about Jesus' lordship and the integrity of God's Word. I believe pastors can and should preach on more than the absolutes, but the congregations need to understand what they're doing.

When I'm teaching on an absolute, I say, "The Bible says...."

When transitioning into an interpretation, I say, "I believe this means...," or, "Many Bible scholars believe...."

If I am teaching a deduction, I usually say something like, "From these Scripture verses we conclude. .."

As the congregation hears these distinctions, they realize the body of Christ includes all who believe the same absolutes, though individuals may differ in interpretations or deductions.

But if people learn that the only true Christians are those who share their interpretations and deductions, then they must exclude from their Christian fellowship practically everyone. Not only would they avoid networking with other churches, but they probably couldn't talk to most of the people in their own church!

We must all resist the temptation to teach or even imply that our deductions have equal importance with absolutes. Now I realize no one teaches material knowing it is untrue. But I don't know anyone who reflects on his own opinions from ten years earlier who would agree with everything he believed, except, of course, for the absolutes.

Subjective Values

What role do subjective values play? Unfortunately, most people use subjective values to choose their local church. That's acceptable only as long as the church is grounded in the absolutes. I suspect that even though some people may say the Lord led them to one church or another, it is often a matter of their being comfortable in the cultural setting a particular church affords them. In some cases they have come to believe a certain setting is "where God is" because of their cultural expectations.

The church I pastor has its own culture. It feels somewhat like an international convention center. All types of people attend, from those who wear cut-off shorts, sandals and tank tops to those who wear very expensive suits and dresses.

Many economic, educational and ethnic groups are represented in our congregation. There is no choir loft, steeple or stained glass.

Some people feel comfortable at New Life Church, while others feel more comfortable in a traditional setting.

Every one of us has a cultural norm that we use as a standard for our Christian worship and study. These cultural norms are not necessarily biblical or contrary to the Bible; they are simply cultural. They are neither good nor bad, as long as we don't equate our religious cultural norms with the essence of our faith.

Heaven is our home, and earth is our mission target. So we must be willing to understand and work within the culture. At the same time, we need to caution against integrating our own cultural heritage with the absolutes of the Scriptures. When we recognize this, it's easier to work with others who have different worship styles than we do because we know our differences are culturally influenced.

Our Primary Purpose

Inside the walls of our churches, let's teach and practice the full menu of what we believe. Let's fully enjoy the security of the absolutes. Let's express and practice our interpretations and deductions. In addition, let's rejoice in our cultural and personal preferences in worship and teaching.

But outside the walls of the church, I believe we must focus on the absolutes. Because when we do, we put tremendous pressure on the forces of evil that want to divide us and distract us from our primary purpose.

The result is that the non-Christian community hears the same basic absolutes from thousands of Christians from a variety of churches. They start wondering where all the Christians have come from. In their viewpoint many people are talking about how wonderful Christ is and how great the Bible is. No longer are they hearing that Baptists are better than Presbyterians or that charismatics are more spiritual than Lutherans. They hear, instead, from all of those groups that Jesus is the only solution to the problems they face and that they can trust the Bible.

The absolutes of the Scripture are what the world needs. Once people come to Christ and into our churches, then they can make choices about interpretations, deductions and culture.

The churches in Colorado Springs were typical of those in many cities, not only in the United States, but also internationally. I believe Christians and non-Christians alike are fed up with judgmental remarks about other churches and Christians and what they believe. They get excited, instead, when they see church leaders and members of different churches working together. That's how principle No. 2 gets put into practice.

Five

PROMOTING THE MINISTRY OF CHRIST AND HIS WORD ABOVE OUR OWN MISSION OR METHOD

(The second of five principles)

W e've all seen the church ads that tout "best choir," "friendliest pastor" or "new sanctuary." Do we want to convince the world that our church or our style is better than all others? Or do we want to work in harmony with other life-giving churches to convince as many as possible that Jesus is alive?

People say, "Come to the men's meeting at our church; it's the best one in the city," or, "Such and such church has the best youth pastor."

Why are we so comparative?

Sometimes we unknowingly encourage this type of comparative thinking. We communicate that our church teaches correct doctrine and has the most complete understanding on any given subject. But sometimes we don't realize the confusion we create. Most people are exposed to other fine Christians who radically differ from us on some interpretations, deductions or subjective values. Even worse is the message that is communicated to non-Christians: "If Christians can't agree with other Christians, how can I trust them with my eternal life?"

A Luxury We Can't Afford

Never forget: the church is in a battle. Your city may not have the overt occult activity that we saw in Colorado Springs, but you can be sure that Satan is using some other strategy to make it hard to go to heaven from your city. It may be pornography, rampant crime, poverty, prosperity, apathy, self-righteousness, religion or any other snare.

In the pre-1960s Judeo-Christian culture of America, the church forgot its primary purpose. We became secure and believed that comparing ourselves among ourselves was a significant task because everyone was a "Christian." And, to some degree, it was true. God-consciousness was reinforced by prayer in schools, at athletic events and during graduation ceremonies. Political leaders would often refer to the Lord and their dependence on God's sovereignty.

During those years, the average American community only had Christian churches. Sometimes a small Jewish synagogue would be present, but there were no Islamic mosques or Hindu temples. The vast majority of people were either Methodist, Baptist, Presbyterian, Mennonite or some other mainline Christian group.

The problem was, though, that the Christian message was losing impact on society because the church became so consumed with itself. We lost our concern for our primary purpose and allowed ourselves to be distracted.

Now America is different. Islam is the fastest-growing religion in several American cities. Hinduism is being taught in our schools and exercise centers. There is no standard of right and wrong — everything is "relative" now. Secular thought is respected; religious thought is scorned. Humanism is the state-sponsored religion, and those who challenge it are ridiculed.

In some Christian circles believers don't even accept the fact that America has changed. In fact, many times we actually use our churches to protect a culture that is long gone. Rather than rethinking our methods and challenging our own effectiveness, we try to escape responsibility for the eternal damnation of those in our communities by blaming others for our own spiritual ineffectiveness.

But we Christians no longer have the luxury of spending time talking about the differences between us. We are losing our cities. We just haven't realized it yet because our church buildings are still standing, and we are so busy doing good things. But being busy has nothing to do with whether or not we have any impact on our cities.

Several times every week I have to ask myself: Is what I'm doing really something that will make a difference in someone else's eternal destiny? Does it pass the "who cares" test? Does it promote Christ and His Word in our community? Will it help the non-Christians in the community understand the message of Christ?

It doesn't matter how great my program, church or actions are in comparison to those of any other Christian. My mission is to communicate a timeless message in a changing culture.

The Cultural Wall

Most non-Christians aren't listening to Christian radio stations or watching Christian television programs. They don't understand Christian jargon, and they don't care about most Christian squabbles. There's a cultural wall between "us" and "them."

I believe we Christians often fail to communicate to non-Christians because we are broadcasting on a different channel. Non-Christians do, however, know when they are hurting and need help.

We recently invited an evangelist named Dave Roever to speak at our church. Dave had fought in the Vietnam War and nearly died when a grenade exploded in his hand. He was horribly burned, and his face had to be almost completely reconstructed. Dave tells people about the absolutes — that Jesus helps you live through all the circumstances of life.

We decided to use radio advertising to announce that Dave was coming. We could have produced an ad just for Christian stations that talked about what a great speaker he was and how he had spoken at many other huge gatherings of Christians. But instead we produced an ad that would also work on secular radio stations that played country and Western, oldies or rock. It told about Dave, but, more importantly, it described how his message could help hurting people.

As a result, people in the secular world could hear about Dave Roever and ask their Christian co-workers about him. The Christian audience would still have an opportunity to hear about the meeting when the ad was played on the Christian radio station. But their attendance would be a by-product of reaching the secular community.

When Dave Roever spoke, the atmosphere was electric because there were so many people attending who did not usually attend church. Christians were excited because their non-Christian friends came with them. And, as you might imagine, the response at the end of Dave's talk was overwhelming. Why? Because the cultural wall had been breached. The special speaker had a practical appeal to non-Christians, and Christians could capitalize on the opportunity to reach their friends because the message was placed within the secular world.

Advertising on a secular station costs more because it reaches more people, but that's the point — to reach people, especially those who aren't saved. I think advertising within the Christian community has its place, but I don't think it should be the primary way we reach new people for our churches. An ad on the religion page will help a few people who are looking for special events or would like to find a new church home, but it doesn't make much of a dent in our primary purpose.

We Christians have built a cultural wall that non-Christians don't understand, so we need to overcome it as often as possible.

The Proactive Message Leaps Over the Cultural Wall

Comparative advertising encourages Christians to go from one church to the other.

Proactive advertising brings the gospel to unsaved people.

A pastor friend told me that his church promotional materials were already proactive. "Well, let's look at them," I said.

He spent his entire promotional budget on Christian radio and television. His television ads said that his church offered "exciting services with practical, relevant Bible teaching."

Since he placed these ads on Christian television, he was really saying, "My church is more exciting than the one you go to," which is an encouragement to leave your church and begin attending his. If he placed these ads on secular radio, he would need to explain what "exciting services" means since most non-Christians can't even imagine what they view as "exciting" going on inside a church.

He also said that the church offered "practical, relevant Bible teaching" without realizing that this implies that the teaching of other churches is inferior. Furthermore, are secular people looking for "practical, relevant Bible teaching"? No, they're looking for purpose in their lives, answers to their problems at work and ways to keep their families together.

69

When designing promotional material for either the Christian or the non-Christian markets, I don't think churches need to compare themselves to other groups. They can focus on the absolutes instead. That way, when Christians from Bible-believing churches hear a radio ad, for example, they will be edified. And when non-Christians hear the ad, they will be encouraged to trust the Lord and His Word. The name of the sponsoring church should be mentioned but not emphasized — because it is not the point.

Since the church name is mentioned, Christians who need to transfer churches have some information to use in making that difficult decision, but they have not been enticed to do so.

An example of proactive advertising is this ad that New Life Church ran on our local country and Western station early in the morning.

> Hi, everybody. This is Pastor Ted from New Life. I know you're busy trying to get ready for work and get the kids off to school, but I just wanted to encourage you to read your Bible for just a minute or two before you leave for work this morning.
>
> The Bible includes great information on how to have a successful marriage, how to raise children, how to have a successful career and even how to balance your budget. The Bible will help your relationship with your supervisor and your co-workers today. Trust me: If you invest just a few minutes in reading your Bible before you leave your house today, you'll have a better day for it.

When we reach the world, we also reach the church. If we target those already in church, we are in effect tempting Christians to become disgruntled.

Pastors describe "flaky" Christians as those who cannot make and keep commitments to themselves or to others. I believe, by example and through our messages, we pastors have taught believers to think like this. Our comparative messages teach Christians to value the wrong things while proactive speech forces all of us to focus on absolutes.

No one cares about my face or what my church looks like. I cannot meet their needs — only Jesus can. I as the pastor am a signpost to point people to Christ, so I am not the person to be promoted. Only Jesus offers everlasting comfort and healing; His Word provides the direction.

Most churches and pastors would never consciously promote a person instead of the gospel. But it often happens in the way the church presents itself to the public. The key is to focus on the absolutes instead of the church or pastor.

New Life church also did some proactive promotion on billboards and bus signs. On the next page are examples of those signs. Notice how the message is "Jesus," while the name of the church is presented inconspicuously.

Secular Media

While I was a youth pastor at Bethany World Prayer Center in Baker, Louisiana, I scheduled a rock music seminar.

On the night of the seminar, cars were backed up for two miles in three directions. The building was full, the parking lot gridlocked and the road filled with miles of cars trying to get in.

CBS taped the church's activities, interviewed students and adults, and collected sound bites for the evening news. Why? Because the Peters Brothers were giving a rock music seminar.

What? Since when did that kind of thing attract so much attention?

When I scheduled the seminar with the Peters Brothers, we decided to promote the multimedia event among the people who enjoyed rock music the most. We paid to have

Need a New Start?

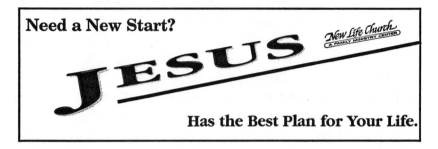

New Life Church
A FAMILY MINISTRY CENTER

Has the Best Plan for Your Life.

Problems?

New Life Church
A FAMILY MINISTRY CENTER

Is <u>the</u> Solution.

Problems?

New Life Church
A FAMILY MINISTRY CENTER

He Will <u>Always</u> Be Faithful to You.

Uncontrollable Habits?
Uncontrollable Thoughts?
Uncontrollable Sex Life?
Uncontrollable Drinking?

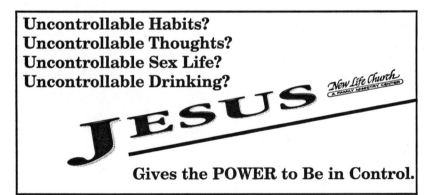

New Life Church
A FAMILY MINISTRY CENTER

Gives the POWER to Be in Control.

the top rock D.J.s make spots that offered the secrets to the lyrics and music of the most popular groups. The top rock stations ran advertisements inviting people to attend.

So, many students from local public schools responded, and many came to Christ. Even the students who weren't Christians stopped listening to secular rock and started buying Christian tapes for their vehicles. The gospel message had effectively penetrated the cultural wall; the lives of thousands of students were transformed. CBS even thought it newsworthy!

Sometimes we wonder why the secular news media never cover our major Christian events. We are tempted to believe that it is because of an anti-Christian bias. I don't think so. I think it is because our events don't touch their world.

Amendment 2 gave Colorado Springs the opportunity to communicate the gospel on the other side of the cultural wall. Bill Moyers, NBC, National Public Radio, the British Broadcasting Corporation, the International News Network and numerous newspapers interviewed me and other Christians about the growth of the Christian community in our city.

The news crews who came to tape these spots were amazed at New Life Church. (It is important to understand that New Life Church is a very typical, independent charismatic church. It has lively worship, strong teaching and altar ministry.) These reporters, though, had never seen anything like it. NBC called it a phenomenon. BBC said they were sure there wasn't another group like it in the world. They, obviously, were very wrong. But in their worldview there was no such thing as a culturally relevant group of believers. Why? Because the church has not penetrated their world.

The cultural wall must be penetrated. We must be in the world. Our message is for them.

Regularly we buy thirty-second spots of television time

and place proactive advertisements on secular programming. We try to place some spots on the filthiest programs we can find. Occasionally, though, we also advertise on children's programs, sports or news programs.

Impact Productions in Tulsa, Oklahoma, has produced two series of thirty-second spots that relate to loneliness, divorce, life after death and so on. They make these spots available to churches throughout the country and have received positive responses from places where they have been used. We have used these spots for years with great effectiveness.

We also produce some of our own spots from time to time. One was filmed in a bar and titled "No More Lonely Nights." One couple saw this spot while they were watching TV together in a bar.

"I hate that spot," the man joked with his date.

"I do too," she replied.

But within a few weeks they ended up at New Life Church and gave their lives to Christ; now the husband is our Promise Keepers ministry coordinator. If that spot had not been on a secular TV program being aired in a bar, we wouldn't have had access to this couple — because they were living on the other side of the cultural wall.

Stop Keeping Count

Remember the *JESUS* video project? Ninety-six different churches went around Colorado Springs giving away videotapes about Jesus. Some pastors wanted to figure out how many new people came to their churches because of their effort. I had no idea. But I knew my church was growing.

So was Woodman Valley Chapel.

And Village Seven Presbyterian.

And Briargate Baptist and hundreds of other local churches.

In fact, I'm glad no one could say how many new people

came to any particular church from that effort. Because if we just counted people in our own churches, we missed the point. I could tell, however, that where we prayed and distributed videos, Christian activity increased across the board.

In other words, we could see that Christ and His Word had been promoted. But we couldn't break it down into particular missions or methods.

That's called raising the water level of the Holy Spirit's activity in your city, and I'll tell you exactly how it works in the next chapter.

Six

Pray to Raise the "Water Level" of the Holy Spirit's Activity in Your City

(The third of five principles)

In the same way that water levels in a reservoir change according to the time of year or amount of rainfall, so cities and regions experience varying levels of the Holy Spirit's activity.

One indication of the Holy Spirit's activity is an increase in the number of active Christians in an area. When a Christian is active, he or she will attend a church. Therefore, we can measure the "water level" of the Holy Spirit's activity in a city by looking at the percentage of people who are attending life-giving churches on an average Sunday morning.

If 10 percent of your city's population are in life-giving churches on Sunday morning, you could graph the water level at 10 percent. By praying to increase the water level of the Holy Spirit's activity in your city by 5 percent in the next year, you would be praying for the Holy Spirit to draw, save and fill an additional 5 percent of the people in your city, bringing the water level to 15 percent, as shown below.

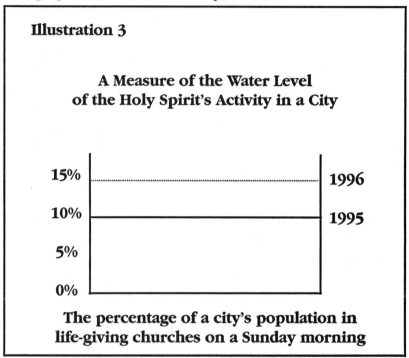

Illustration 3

A Measure of the Water Level of the Holy Spirit's Activity in a City

The percentage of a city's population in life-giving churches on a Sunday morning

Colorado Springs has a population of approximately three hundred thousand, and there are about two hundred life-giving churches in the area. In order to raise the water level 5 percent in a year, fifteen thousand more people would need to attend these churches. That is an average growth of seventy-five people in each of the two hundred churches. That is possible!

But if I prayed for the church that I pastor to increase by fifteen thousand people in one year, the likelihood of that happening would be slim.

Spheres of Influence

The squares in the illustration on the next page represent your city. The circles represent the spheres of influence of local life-giving churches. Those citizens inside the spheres of influence are able to hear the gospel and receive eternal life. The space between the spheres of influence represent the people in the community that do not have relationships that allow them easy access to a personal gospel witness.

City B demonstrates what would happen if your church tripled in the next year. Although a 300 percent growth rate would be remarkably impressive, note that it doesn't make a major difference in the number of people who can hear the gospel message. One church experiencing phenomenal growth does not make it that much harder to go to hell from your city.

But City C demonstrates the effect of all the life-giving churches doubling their spheres of influence. When that happens, the area outside the influence of a life-giving gospel message becomes dramatically smaller. When this type of growth occurs, newly planted churches greatly assist the life-giving churches in reaching areas of the community still beyond their spheres of influence. Just a few years of universal church growth in the life-giving churches is the only genuine way I know of to make it hard to go to hell from your city and create the societal shifts necessary to reflect a strong gospel impact.

Church growth in many life-giving churches is the best way to make it hard to go to hell from your city.

Prayer

When I pray and fast, I like to rent a room with a couple of friends in an area where we can go on prayer walks through neighborhoods. Our goal is to raise the water level

Illustration 4

Increasing the Influence of the Church in a City

CITY A

Most of the population lives outside the influence of any life-giving church.

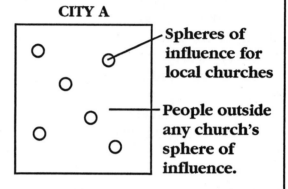

Spheres of influence for local churches

People outside any church's sphere of influence.

CITY B

Growth in only one church leaves much of the city still unreached.

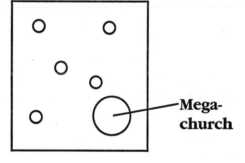

Mega-church

CITY C

Growth in all life-giving churches makes it difficult to avoid the gospel.

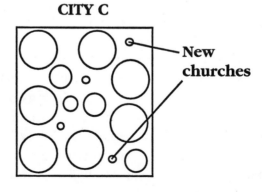

New churches

of the Holy Spirit's activity in that region. As we walk through the neighborhood praying, we pray for the people who live in the homes we pass by. We pray for the businesses we come across and for God's blessing on every church we walk past.

We sometimes don't know anything specific about the churches we come across, so we pray in a way that we would appreciate others praying for us. We walk around the church asking God to bless all of those who worship there. We war against any demonic spirits working against the church or the individuals who attend. We ask God to bless them financially, encourage their vision, increase their passion and add more families to their church body.

We take oil, as a symbol of the Holy Spirit, and place it at the corners of the church buildings. We anoint the doorposts and the perimeter of the property. We stand as intercessors, asking God for great miracles.

If we happen to know that the church we are praying for is not life-giving, we are responsible to become aggressive spiritual warriors. We pray for the revelation of Scriptures and the power of the Holy Spirit to be manifest at these churches. We pray for a personal encounter with the Lord that will change them into life-giving churches.

We are always careful not to draw attention to ourselves or to appear threatening. If we feel awkward, we'll just pray discreetly while walking by the front of the church at a normal pace. Our purpose is not to be seen but to increase the water level of the Holy Spirit's activity in the region.

Based on some information gathered by the Colorado Springs Association of Evangelicals, I estimate that 17 percent of the population of Colorado Springs attended life-giving churches on an average Sunday morning in 1994. Ten years ago I believe only 10 percent of Colorado Springs attended life-giving churches. I am praying that within the next five years, 25 percent of our city will attend life-giving churches.

When we start to pray in terms of raising the water level, it confuses demonic resistance and opens the door to greater manifestations of God's kingdom. It also helps us realize that other people's successes are not a threat because as the water level increases in the region, our own ministries will increase as well. It's obviously a win-win situation.

Bubbles of Church Growth

Numbers from the 1980s are forcing us to rethink growth in the church.

During that time we experienced the phenomenal growth of the mega-churches and the large parachurch ministries. (I define a mega-church as one having regular attendance of over 1 percent of the city's population.) As churches and ministries were growing, we thought that the gospel message was reaching a greater percentage of people from that region. But in many cases overall church attendance was declining.

A mega-church is like a bubble or a wave in the water level of a community (See Illustration 5).

In order to sustain a bubble like this over time, the water level around the bubble needs to be increased.

It takes a tremendous amount of energy to maintain a bubble over an extended period of time. In many cases, the bubble churches of one decade become the average church of the next.

Rather than spending excessive energy maintaining the large church, efforts should be made to raise the water level around the bubble, thus allowing it to stay large easily, or become an even larger church. But to try to make the church larger without raising the entire water level in the community is ultimately fruitless.

For example, right now in Colorado Springs, New Life Church is disproportionately larger than most other churches

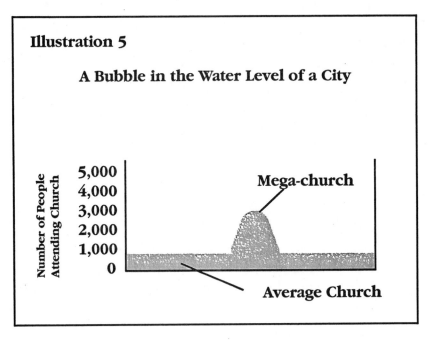

Illustration 5

A Bubble in the Water Level of a City

in the region. I want New Life Church to grow even larger because of the reality of heaven and hell. But to embrace growth and sustain it, we must pray and work together to encourage other churches in the region to grow.

If a city has several life-giving churches with a Sunday attendance of three thousand, then a bubble of a church of six thousand on Sundays could be sustained. But if the other large churches have only five hundred people, it would be difficult for one church to maintain a consistent Sunday attendance of six thousand.

Considering the position I'm in, I'm obviously an advocate for mega-churches. God is blessing the Christian community with mega-churches and large parachurch ministries because He loves the lost. Mega-churches have a great accumulation of resources and prayer power that could transform cities — if their people don't make one crucial mistake.

The Role of the Mega-Churches

The mega-church must not be deceived into thinking its growth means impact if, in reality, its resources become diluted. Let me illustrate.

As a church grows, decisions have to be made about the most effective ways to spend money to reach people. The budgets of most large local churches go toward buildings and staff. If excessive debt or exorbitant salaries don't become a problem, churches also have the opportunity to decide how to spend money on outreach. At New Life Church we have made fundamental decisions about our outreach resources:

1. To concentrate our resources to produce measurable results for the kingdom of God in our region.

2. To finance missions projects that raise the water level of the Holy Spirit's activity in areas of the world where the people who live there could never do it themselves.

Many churches make a major mistake by investing all their outreach money on nationwide programs that minister primarily to the Christian culture. That investment will not have a concentrated impact on any one geographical area and probably won't make any measurable difference. Because they get some response, they know they are reaching and helping people. But because their resources are spread so thin, they are, in actuality, contributing to the fact that their own city is declining spiritually.

A pastor could take thirty-five thousand dollars per month and buy national radio or TV time. Or a church could invest the same thirty-five thousand dollars in their region communicating the gospel through local media and community service.

In the first scenario the pastor may become well-known and could demonstrate success by increased income, growing mailing lists and additional opportunities — all producing wonderful testimonial letters. But, in the midst of a growing ministry, it is doubtful that they could point to any specific city where their influence contributed to a measurable decline in crime rates, growth in overall church attendance or any other societal adjustment.

A mega-church will make a lasting impact if it puts definite geographical boundaries on its ministry. When we maintain boundaries, we accumulate water and have a massive reservoir of strength with which to communicate the gospel to everyone in our population area. It's like the water that builds up behind a dam. But if the boundaries aren't there, the water becomes shallow, and the impact is diluted.

Transfer or Conversion Growth

Some church activities create a stir but make no eternal difference. A good example is transfer growth.

Transfer growth occurs when people move from one church to another but make no overall improvement in the water level of the Holy Spirit's activity in a city (see Illustration 6). The only positive impact of transfer growth is when a person switches from a nonbelieving church to a life-giving church. Sometimes transfer growth occurs when Christians move into town and are looking for a new church home. At other times, however, another church may not have adequately met their felt needs, so they choose to switch churches.

The illusion of the past says, "If my church is growing, then it is making a difference in our city." The reality is that if one life-giving church grows because another is declining, then there is no net difference in the social and cultural makeup of the city.

Conversion growth is much more difficult, but it makes

an immediate improvement in the water level of the Holy Spirit's activity in a city. It requires reaching into the nonchurched community with the gospel message and discipling those who respond to the Lord.

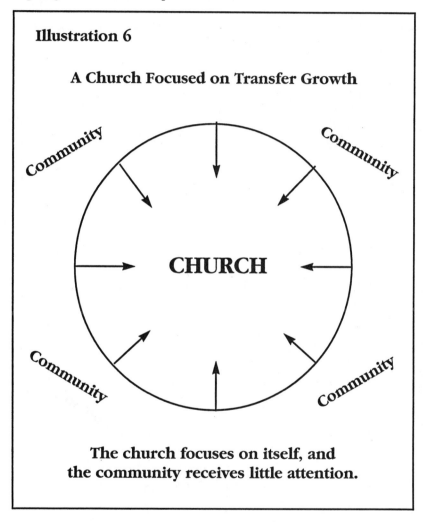

Illustration 6

A Church Focused on Transfer Growth

CHURCH

Community
Community
Community
Community

**The church focuses on itself, and
the community receives little attention.**

If we focus on transfer growth in our prayers, thoughts and actions, we focus upon ourselves. We pray, think and act in terms of self-preservation and self-promotion. Comparative thinking and speaking are the norm.

In contrast, people in churches that emphasize conversion growth intentionally focus on serving and encouraging the unchurched. Proactive and creative thinking and praying are required. Attention goes outward to the community (see Illustration 7).

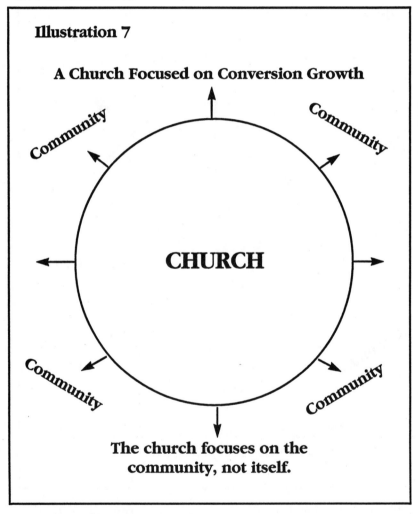

Illustration 7

A Church Focused on Conversion Growth

CHURCH

Community Community Community Community

The church focuses on the community, not itself.

Some transfer growth will occur as a natural by-product of working for conversion growth. It is a healthy and necessary development, but it cannot be the focus of our efforts.

On an average Sunday morning, the congregation at New Life Church is made up of about 50 percent transfers from other churches and about 50 percent people who were either born-again or have recommitted their lives to Christ in our church. That means we have made a legitimate contribution to raising the water level of the Holy Spirit's activity in our city. If our church was comprised predominantly of transfer members, it would indicate that we hadn't made a significant difference in the social or cultural balance of the city.

My job right now is to do all I can to encourage the growth of other life-giving churches in our region and to raise the water level of the Holy Spirit's activity in Colorado Springs. As this happens, all of us grow; we have greater opportunities; and our city is effectively reached for the cause of the kingdom.

The Colorado Initiative

Last year we decided to start praying to raise the water level of the Holy Spirit's activity in the entire state of Colorado. We knew God had wonderful believers and churches all over the state, so we decided we would quietly attempt to undergird the body of Christ statewide through servant-minded warfare prayer.

We asked people from our church to adopt the sixty-three counties in our state. Each team took a county and met four times to pray for it. Then they took a prayer journey to their county to pray on-site (with pastors of local churches whenever possible). Then, after returning, the teams met to pray four more times.

I have received phone calls from pastors whose churches increased their attendance only weeks after prayer teams visited their communities. These were often churches from small communities in the Rocky Mountains or in the eastern plains of the state. Often Christians in these communities feel alone and forgotten — certainly off the beaten path. But after a day of praying with a prayer team, they are so excited about what God is going to do that their church naturally grows.

Because increases in the kingdom of God in Colorado Springs coincided with lower crime rates, it would make sense that increases in the kingdom of God throughout the state of Colorado would reduce crime at the state level. I am confident that as statistics become available for the state of Colorado, we are going to see a similar trend state wide — increased church participation and lower crime rates.

When we pray to raise the water level of the Holy Spirit's activity in our city, many times we end up praying for ministries that interpret some portions of Scripture differently from the way we interpret them or have a different culture from ours. But they are still life-giving. Therefore we must view our differences as a strength, which means appreciating one another's respected interpretations of Scripture.

Seven

APPRECIATE ONE ANOTHER'S RESPECTED INTERPRETATIONS OF SCRIPTURE

(The fourth of five principles)

During World War II some soldiers had a buddy who died. They went to a local Roman Catholic parish and asked the priest if they could bury their friend in the fenced graveyard beside the church.

The old priest asked, "Was the man Roman Catholic?"

"We haven't any idea," they said.

The priest replied, "Well, you'll have to bury him just outside the graveyard fence then."

So they buried the body outside the fence and left. They happened to pass through the same town later, however, and visited their friend's grave. They looked at the fence in amazement. It wasn't where it had been before. The old priest, realizing that his way of thinking was ungodly, had moved the fence to include the fallen soldier's grave.

Who Loves a Wall?

I told that story at the start of a prayer and fasting retreat for pastors and asked them to think about moving their fences that weekend to include more people in their circle of acceptance.

At the end of the weekend a Baptist pastor told the group through tears, "As I met you and worshipped and prayed with you, I had to start moving my fence. I didn't want to because it was so much easier knowing that my group was right and most of yours weren't. But I realized that you love the Lord and the Bible too. I didn't know that because this is the first time I have gone to anything but Baptist pastors' meetings."

He finished by saying, "As I was moving my fence, it fell down, and I've just decided to leave it that way."

All the pastors in the room cheered!

We often build fences that exclude believers with different interpretations, deductions or opinions from ours. Charismatics look down on those they think aren't as "Spirit-filled" as they are. Mainline denominations look down on charismatics for what they see as haphazard theology. Catholics glory in their long history, while Protestants relish their hyper-individualism. It seems that if we're properly trained, we know exactly whom we are not to associate with because they are not like us.

But that is a horrible misunderstanding. Jesus, the head of the church, uses our differences to reach the lost. Despite the poor way we handle them, the various expressions within the body of Christ are not our shame or failure at all. They are a strength, designed by God to make His body more effective.

I Love Ice Cream Stores

I love all kinds of ice cream. Sometimes I want vanilla

with caramel topping, whipped cream, lots of nuts and a cherry. Other times I want rocky road, banana or chocolate chip. Very seldom do I like plain vanilla, but sometimes perky strawberry sounds good.

That's why I love the Baskin-Robbins ice cream stores. They have thirty-one flavors, and I can always find something I like. All of it is ice cream, but each has a different flavor.

In Colorado Springs we enjoy ninety different flavors of churches. Most of these groups stand on the message of Christ as their cornerstone and embrace the Bible as their authority. So in each of them you could discover the same basic truths that make eternal life available to all.

By discussing various flavors in the body of Christ, I am not speaking of an ecumenical, humanistic movement that embraces all people of all faiths as brothers and sisters. Instead I am saying that we need to appreciate one another's "respected interpretations" of Scripture, which are interpretations that are respected by mainstream biblical scholarship. They are not heresies or teachings that threaten the divinity of Christ or the integrity of His Word.

But I think the Lord planned for local churches to be distinctive for a reason.

Reaching the Lost

Let's say that on Elm Street, USA, there are five Christian churches. Let's also assume each of the pastors has elected to focus on the absolutes of Scripture. One is Presbyterian, another Baptist, another Catholic and another charismatic, and the last one is Methodist.

Joe Schmoe, a nonbeliever, moved to town and heard people speaking positively about the Lord in public. He decided to visit a church. Remember: Joe is a nonbeliever. He is not church-hopping or trying to find a church that will meet his emotional and cultural needs. Instead he is searching for answers. All of our cities are full of people like Joe.

He began by attending the Presbyterian church. Everyone was dressed very nicely and was very polite. Hymns were sung, the choir was impressive, and the pastor explained that Jesus Christ is the only solution to mankind's sin problem. Joe heard the message and enjoyed the service but was a little uncomfortable with the formality.

The next Sunday he visited the charismatic church. Everyone was happy, loud and direct. Music was playing, colors were bright, and the pastor was out in the crowd talking and laughing. When the service began, Joe was completely disoriented. People clapped their hands and jumped with joy, and many played tambourines. It was a wonderful celebration. But he had no idea how the people knew when to lift their hands and close their eyes or clap and jump. Some songs seemed to have hand motions that really baffled him.

When the pastor spoke, he explained the same basic principle the Presbyterian pastor explained: Jesus is the solution to mankind's sin problem. Joe enjoyed the church very much but didn't feel secure. He wanted something that felt a little more traditional.

The next week he moved on to the Catholic church and attended Mass. The priest at this particular Catholic church was a charismatic; he encouraged his parishioners in their personal prayer lives and devotion to the Scriptures. As he delivered the homily, Joe heard about the powerful inner transformation available through a personal encounter with Christ. He heard, once again, about sins being forgiven and the blood of Christ being efficacious for all who repent and believe. Even though the message spoke to him, the culture of the service was a stumbling block to him. He needed something much more relaxed.

The following Sunday, Joe visited the Methodist church. The Sunday school teacher told the story about going on a prayer journey into the 10/40 Window. She recited the events of powerful prayer and engaging intercession. She wanted to begin prayer walks in the community to raise the water level of the Holy Spirit's activity so that more people would experience the love of Jesus in their lives.

Joe's heart was touched. Rather than going to the main worship service, he stayed after the Sunday school class. He prayed with the teacher to accept Christ, and today Joe is a Spirit-filled Methodist.

How did that happen?

He heard the same basic message from the various flavors in the body of Christ. No one tried to convince him that their flavor was the perfect flavor able to meet every need. Instead, all of the flavors, while maintaining their own distinctives, communicated the necessity of Christ.

Strategy From Diversity

The church I pastor is an independent, charismatic church that has a strong international emphasis. Flags from nearly every nation on earth hang from its rafters (because charismatics look at the ceilings of their churches more than any other Christian group I know), making it feel more like a convention center than a church. Our flavor helps us serve a group of people that a traditional Baptist church would not normally reach. The Baptist church, though, can serve people our church could never reach.

Bottom line: Our primary purpose does not require every church to reach every person. It would be impossible. God would not allow it because it would violate His establishment of the body. Instead God requires us to reach a specific group effectively and helps us understand that a different flavor in the body of Christ is our co-worker to reach still another group. Through the strength we draw from our different flavors, we can communicate to the various people within our communities.

Humility Helps

Humility is required.

I've had many people say something like this to me: "Pastor Ted, we love you and New Life, but our family is going to start attending Pulpit Rock church because their youth program appeals to our children. We don't want to hurt your feelings, but we think our family will grow more in that church."

As my heart sinks and I feel a little abandoned, my first thought is: I'm investing my life in this thing, and they flippantly come and go. Then I remind myself that both churches are working to serve people; the people don't have to serve us. So I thank them for their involvement while here and comfort myself knowing that they are, indeed, transferring to a life-giving church — just of a different flavor.

It may be easy to say that we respect other ministries, but it takes humility to practice it.

Learning From Others

When I came to Colorado Springs, I had never been a senior pastor of a church before. But I realized that I was repeating a mistake I had seen in most of the churches where I had been involved. I failed to cultivate servant/leaders from within my congregation.

After a long discussion with a Presbyterian pastor, I saw that my cultural history in the church left me with very little appreciation or understanding of the biblical role of elders in a local church. After reading his material and having extensive talks with my Presbyterian brother, I spoke to our church on eldership and identified a group of elders who could assist me and the other members of the pastoral team in serving our church body.

I could never have learned that lesson from my own flavor in the body of Christ. Even though we are all ice cream, we need the variety of flavors.

Eight

PRACTICE SUPPORTIVE SPEECH AND ACTIONS TOWARD OTHERS

(The fifth of five principles)

In a small town in Louisiana, I saw one of the finest examples of "supportive speech and action" I have ever seen.

A small downtown church had been in the community for years. Then a local Baptist pastor started a new church on the edge of the city, with very charismatic services.

As the Baptist church grew, the pastor of the smaller church was vehement. "There's a church on the other side of town full of false doctrine," he preached. "There are demonic things going on over there. Just stay away because you never know what could happen to you."

But the Spirit-filled Baptists grew from one large building

to an even larger one. Their youth group became larger than the entire congregation at the other church.

This went on for fifteen years. The smaller congregation continued to shrink, and their little white frame building fell into disrepair. The Baptist church, on the other hand, was in new, well-maintained buildings and getting new, young families all the time.

Finally, the smaller church's building became unsafe. If they couldn't get the money to repair it, they would have to close. By this time the congregation was down to thirty people. Money was scarce.

The pastor of the Baptist church heard about the problems of the church that had been preaching against him for so long. He immediately contacted the other pastor and explained that his church would like to help them. What did they need?

Within a month the Baptist church paid for the old church to be torn down and built a brand new brick building on the same spot for the body of elderly believers.

As you can imagine, that generous act changed the heart of the traditional pastor. He stopped preaching against the Baptist church, even though they continued to be of a different flavor. He even started bragging about what good Christian people they were.

The body of Christ in the entire city was strengthened because of supportive speech and actions.

Respect Spiritual Authority

When I first arrived in Colorado Springs, the potential existed for me to have my own standoff with a local pastor.

Before I arrived, the Village Seven Presbyterian Church took a very public position regarding some of the loose theology taught in charismatic circles. This was a major blow to some of the smaller charismatic churches and to those who believed in the modern-day operation of the gifts.

About the time that announcement was made at Village

Seven, we were a small storefront church, and God was dealing with me about spiritual authority. I had been reading Gene Edwards's *A Tale of Three Kings*, Watchman Nee's *Spiritual Authority* and material from Bill Gothard. The ideas in the three combined sources made a huge impact on me.

As I prayed over the city, I received a strong impression that I had limited authority and that I needed to honor those in the city whom God had chosen to honor. I asked Him who the spiritual leaders of the city were, and Bernie Kuiper, the non-charismatic pastor of Village Seven Presbyterian Church, came to mind.

I made an appointment with Dr. Kuiper. When I met with him I explained that I believed he was chosen by God as a spiritual leader in the city and I would always speak respectfully and honorably about him. He asked me several questions regarding charismatic theology and, I believe, was pleasantly surprised by my answers. Then we prayed together for our churches and our city.

Not long after that, volunteers from several churches met together at Radiant Assembly of God to organize the phone counseling for the Will Perkins television spots that would air at Christmas. Dr. Kuiper and I were both there to speak and encourage people to participate. Instead of speaking one at a time, we stood at the front together and talked about how exciting it was to see new people come to Jesus.

I guess talking about people getting saved loosened us up a bit. Laughing, we agreed that if anyone went to Village Seven and got too emotional, Dr. Kuiper would send them to New Life. And if anyone came to New Life in a suit that cost more than fifteen hundred dollars, we would send them to Village Seven. The crowd laughed and applauded.

I think they loved seeing two pastors put aside their differences and work together for the spiritual health of a city. I have warmly referred to Dr. Kuiper as "bishop" ever since, and our relationship is now one of mutual respect and warm friendship.

It Doesn't Hurt to Talk

A group of representatives from various spiritual backgrounds in Colorado Springs began meeting bi-monthly in 1993 to develop relationships with one another. The group now includes Rabbi Howard Hirsch from Temple Shalom, Bishop Richard Hanifen from the Roman Catholic diocese, James Dobson from Focus on the Family, James White from First Congregational (United Church of Christ), Terry Taylor from the Navigators, others and me.

Our time together has allowed us to establish a foundation of respect. After a few months of meetings, we started to become friends. Our common ground is the fact that all of us worship the God of Israel and have a deep conviction that people should be both respectful and respected.

As a result, the group members signed a Covenant of Mutual Respect. We distributed it in our churches and printed it in the newspaper on a full-page ad so the community could see it. The second paragraph of the covenant reads:

> The diversity of our religious perspectives may lead us into areas of possible disagreement. It is our hope to address those areas of difference with an attitude of openness, respect and love, and a willingness to listen and learn from each other, to the end that we may manifest the ministry of reconciliation. With this hope and prayer before us, we covenant together to conduct our common life by the scriptural standards of justice, mercy, righteousness and peace as we provide leadership in our congregations, organizations and community. We believe that in so doing we reflect the nature of our God — the Creator of the universe and Lord of all!

This covenant has helped create close friendships among

the groups. Now, whenever any of our flavors is involved in a major project, there is a friendly, supportive climate that allows free, open discussions and personal security for all of us.

Dare to Like People You Disagree With

The Catholic Diocese of Colorado Springs recently hosted a Congress on Reconciliation, Healing and Hospitality. We discussed the questions "What Drives Us Apart?" and "What Brings Us Together?" The two guest speakers were Robert Bellah, author of *Habits of the Heart* and *The Good Society,* and Margaret O'Brien Steinfels, author of *Who's Minding the Children: The History and Politics of Day Care in America,* both social liberals.

To complement these major speakers was a panel of guest speakers from our community. They included Clair Garcia, an African-American English professor from Colorado College; Howard Hirsch, rabbi of Temple Shalom and professor of religion at Regis College; Mary Lou Makepeace, the senior member of the Colorado Springs city council; and me.

We represented a broad variety of responses to the presentations given by the main speakers. We attend different places of worship. We embrace differing political positions. We have competing views on many social/political/spiritual issues — but *we are all friends.* We honestly enjoy and respect one another — we honor one another. We have the opportunity to communicate ideas to one another so the Catholic community has a wholesome understanding of the heart of the conservative evangelical.

In any free society it is important for ideas to flow freely. I know the events of the gospel are the grandest events in history. I know there is a God in heaven, and He has definite opinions. I also know that the people who live in our city believe what they believe for a reason. And I should hear and understand those reasons.

I am not fearful of liking people who don t agree with me on everything.

Treat People as if You're Going to Need Them Someday

The front page of the Sunday morning paper had a huge color picture of me in our church auditorium. Above my head were three ten-by-ten foot screens on which we project the words to our songs and our announcements. And on the screens were the names of each of our county commissioners. The headline over the article read "Religion and Politics."

The article never explained why the names of the county commissioners were on our projection screens. But it did talk in general terms about how religious organizations were influencing politics. So the impression was that I was a political activist and used the Sunday morning service to coach the congregation about our county commissioners.

But on that particular Sunday morning, we as a congregation were filling out our annual prayer guides. On one page of that prayer guide we needed to fill in the names of the county commissioners. So I had arranged to have the names projected on the screen so that people could copy them down.

The minute that newspaper hit the streets, the newspaper offices started getting responses — first from people who had attended the service and knew what the names were there for; then from the people in town who had a relationship with me or the church. It was heartwarming when the Jewish community, the Catholic community, and the conservative and liberal Protestant community defended New Life. They all communicated: What you said about New Life was not true!

The newspaper printed a retraction by Wednesday.

Exercise Wisdom

Speaking respectfully and thoughtfully about others can never hurt us. Jack Hayford's attitude toward John MacArthur is a blessing to the body of Christ. (Jack is charismatic and John is anticharismatic.) But if Jack began saying negative things about John, the body of Christ overall would be hurt.

Now I'm not saying we should be spineless creatures fearful of taking strong positions. I don't think either Jack Hayford or John MacArthur is spineless. They maintain their positions — but are respectful.

So it is with New Life Church and Village Seven Presbyterian and Temple Shalom and the Catholic diocese. I am an Armenian charismatic. I do not accept all reformed theology; I believe firmly that Jesus is the Messiah; and I do not accept Rome as the authority for the church. At the same time, I respect reformed theology; I love my Jewish friends; and I have great appreciation for Bishop Hanifen, a Roman Catholic, and those who serve with him.

Just Do It

In Colorado Springs there was a small fundamentalist Bible church that was very exclusive. They would print "King James only — noncharismatic" in their newspaper advertisements. For years they taught that no one could be genuinely born again without using the King James Version and that other Bibles and all other churches were prostitutes of the world.

Then this devout congregation found themselves in the middle of a battle over zoning that would have put a pornographic bookstore next to their church. They won, but it cost them a fortune in legal fees.

In the midst of their struggle, I tried on several occasions to call the pastor. He was never available. Then one day when I called, I told the secretary we wanted to help with the legal expenses. The pastor called me back within ten minutes. I asked him how much they still owed and told him New Life Church would send his church the amount needed to pay the balance.

He was very pleased.

I have never spoken with this brother about old texts and modern translations, but I have heard that he no longer preaches that the King James Version is the only Bible God can use to speak to people.

I have never spoken with this brother about cessationist dispensationalism and its contrast to charismatic theology, but he no longer teaches that people who speak in tongues are demonized.

I have never spoken with this brother about the various cultural expressions within the body of Christ, but he no longer teaches that his church's way is the only way to worship.

I think this pastor may have felt as if he didn't have any friends in the Christian community until we made a concrete gesture of friendship. When he realized that other people in the Christian community accepted him, it changed his attitude.

Recently I was in a restaurant when a man approached me. "You're the pastor of New Life, aren't you?" I nodded, and he continued with a big smile. "I just wanted to let you know that I went to your church to see the play 'Heaven's Gates and Hell's Flames.' You have a great church."

Just before he excused himself he mentioned casually which church he attended — the same little church that used to be "King James only" and "anticharismatic."

Spiritual Warfare

Paul says that strongholds are "arguments" and "pretensions" that work against Christ and that they need to be pulled down through divine power (2 Cor. 10:4-5). In other words, strongholds are ideas, thoughts or world views people hold.

Supportive speech and actions toward others negate demonic attempts to build strongholds in our minds against other members of the body of Christ. When we say good things about each other and do good things for each other, we are using spiritual weapons that can break demonic and worldly strongholds. When people are committed to blessing each other, neither the world nor the devil has the power to poison their relationships. Divisiveness, territorialism, bitterness, hatred and jealousy are unable to gain a foothold. As a result, the Holy Spirit has great opportunity to build a strong coalition in the body of Christ that can make a significant impact on our communities.

Spiritual warfare is usually not thought of in these terms. We engage in spiritual warfare while praying — and that is effective. But there are other ways to do spiritual warfare — through our lifestyles.

LIFESTYLE WARFARE

Seven Power Points

Nine

LIVING IN THE TREE OF LIFE

Power Point #1

One Sunday morning after I taught on spiritual warfare, a pleasant young man came up to me after the service to talk.

"Pastor Haggard," he began, "do you think spiritual warfare can help me with pornography?"

"Of course," I replied.

"I'm so glad to hear you say that," he answered. "I struggle with pornography. But whenever I'm in an adult bookstore watching a movie, I rebuke the strongholds of pornography in Jesus' name. That way the demons can't take advantage of me."

He was wrong.

Spiritual warfare is not always just a prayer on your lips. For this brother, spiritual warfare would have been to avoid the adult bookstore and find some believers who would help him stay pure. The act of going to the right place and avoiding the wrong place is as much a part of spiritual warfare as saying a prayer.

Lifestyle Warfare

Spiritual warfare goes beyond the words that we say, though they are essential. Spiritual warfare also takes place when:

- we tell the truth instead of a lie
- we choose to stay faithful to our spouses
- we protect our children
- we encourage instead of judge
- we smile instead of frown
- we treat people with respect
- we serve instead of control

I call these actions *lifestyle warfare* to remind myself that spiritual warfare starts with prayer, but it doesn't end there. I am absolutely convinced that spiritual warfare occurs not only in our prayer closets but also in the way we demonstrate the character of Christ in our daily living.

This principle of lifestyle warfare became clear to me as I thought about the goals of spiritual warfare, which are to:

1. stimulate the activity of the Holy Spirit
2. hinder the work of Satan

What happens when you choose Mountain Dew over Budweiser? You open your heart for the ministry of the Holy Spirit and eliminate demonic opportunities.

What happens when you spend time building relationships with your children? You open hearts for the ministry of the Holy Spirit and eliminate demonic opportunities.

What happens when you honor your boss at work? You open hearts for the ministry of the Holy Spirit and eliminate demonic opportunities.

Lifestyle warfare does four things:

1. Provides opportunity for the ministry of the Holy Spirit

2. Blocks satanic opportunity

3. Earns us the right to be heard in the non-Christian community

4. Makes it hard to go to hell from our cities

Lifestyle warfare reinforced the prayers that went up for Colorado Springs.

What good would it have done if we prayed through the phone book but weren't respectful to our neighbors? People wouldn't have been so open to the gospel because we would not have earned the right to be heard.

What good would it have done if we pulled down a stronghold of control but refused to submit to God's delegated authorities? The stronghold would have reestablished itself.

What good would it have done to pray for more of God's kingdom in Colorado Springs if the Christians in town were known for not paying their bills? People wouldn't have wanted more of that kind of kingdom.

Please don't misunderstand me. I believe that communion with God and confrontation with evil power in prayer are absolutely essential to change a city's spiritual climate. But I know they are much more effective when accompanied by lifestyle warfare.

I think it's like using a spear. Prayer (spiritual warfare) is the tip of the spear, and lifestyle warfare is the shaft.

Throwing the tip of a spear is not very effective. Neither is throwing the shaft. But if you use the spear tip and shaft together, you'll have a powerful weapon.

In the next seven chapters, I am going to describe seven power points of lifestyle warfare. You will discover others as you recognize the impact of your actions in the spiritual world.

Living in the Tree of Life

I was prayer walking through the downtown area of Colorado Springs with the music minister of our church, Ross Parsley, when we came upon a strange-looking building. The front door looked as if it were never used, and the windows were covered. So we went around to the back and found the entrance and a parking lot full of cars.

A man was sitting on a nearby curb, so we asked him what kind of business was there. He told us that it was a gay bar and asked us if we would like to go in with him. After a friendly discussion we declined his offer and continued to walk and pray discreetly for the bar and the people inside.

Two days later I had a meeting scheduled with one of the men of the church. On my way there, I had to go near the intersection where the bar was located and wondered how many cars would be in the parking lot of that bar in the middle of the day. To my surprise, as I drove past the bar's parking lot, I saw a man from my church walking out of the door.

I parked my car quickly, walked up to him in the parking lot and quietly called out his name. He glanced up. Immediately his gaze dropped to the pavement, and he turned his head to the side with shame. I said gently, "Brother, I love you. Jesus sent me here to rescue you."

He burst into tears. After getting into my car and praying together, we called the church counseling office from my car phone and set up an appointment for him immediately.

When I saw this brother coming out of a gay bar, I could have approached him one of two ways: from the tree of life or from the tree of the knowledge of good and evil. If I operated from the tree of the knowledge of good and evil, I would have said something harsh like, "I am so disappointed in you. How long has this been going on? You are living in sin, and you need to repent." He would have been hurt, angry and defensive and would probably have become bitter. My words would have hardened him to redemption and made it hard for any Christian to minister to him.

Instead I spoke to him out of the tree of life: "Brother, I love you. Jesus sent me here to rescue you." I did not condone what he was doing, nor was I sympathetic. I simply offered a way of escape. My purpose was to restore him to life, not pronounce harsh judgment on his actions.

He was faithful to follow through with the counseling and hasn't fallen to that kind of temptation since.

Choices in the Garden

In the garden of Eden, Adam and Eve had a choice between the tree of life and the tree of the knowledge of good and evil. Day after day they lived in the life of God, until the serpent came to Eve and tempted her. She chose the knowledge of good and evil, and her husband did the same (Gen. 2:16-17; 3:1-24). Instead of choosing life, they chose death.

Every day we have a choice between the tree of life and the tree of the knowledge of good and evil.

Living in the tree of life means making choices that will lead to life — in our lives and in the lives of those around us. Living in the tree of the knowledge of good and evil means making choices based on what is good and what is evil — which leads to death in us and possibly in those around us.

As a young man, I could never understand why some

good Christian people could be so mean. Or why some holy people were so angry. Or why churches could be so correct in their doctrine and be so bitter against others — until I understood the difference between the two trees.

You can read the Bible from the tree-of-life perspective and find redemption, healing, trust and peace and live as a man or woman in whom God's kingdom is evident.

Or you can read your Bible from the tree-of-the-knowl-edge-of-good-and-evil perspective and become legalistic and condemn everyone who doesn't agree with you. Unfortunately some miss the point of their Bibles and use God's Word as a vicious weapon of tyranny in other people's lives and in their own lives as well.

For example, let's say that from the tree of the knowledge of good and evil you decide to read your Bible every day because that is a good thing to do. After all, the Bible says to hide the Word in your heart. So you read your Bible every day, but you become arrogant about it. Then when you find somebody who doesn't read the Bible every day, you say, "You ought to read your Bible every day. If you were really a good Christian, you would read your Bible every day."

But reading your Bible every day from the tree of life is totally different because your purpose is different. You're saying, "I love reading the Bible every chance I get. The life of God flows into me as I read my Bible. It makes me want to pray more, and then I pray more, and it makes me want to read my Bible more. I tell you what, the Bible is the greatest thing I have ever found!"

Then when someone tells you that he doesn't read his Bible every day, you say, "Brother, you've got to discover this book! It's a wonderful book; it's a life-giving book; it's a liberating book. It tells you how to have a great marriage and how to have a good business and how to treat people and how to forgive people. The Bible is the way to go."

Living according to the tree of life means you live in a way that brings life to you and others. You do what the Bible says, and you serve other people with joy. You have an attitude of gratefulness because of Jesus' life.

Choosing the tree of knowledge makes you filter everything through a value system of judging what is good and what is evil. Obviously you cannot find His life in knowing what is good and evil. If you're an expert on what is good, you will judge yourself and others so harshly that you will die. If you're an expert on evil, corruption will creep into your heart and kill you. Knowledge of good and evil always has the same result: death.

That's why Jesus wants us to choose His life.

Safe to Be Rescued

Jesus wants us to have the kinds of churches where He can rescue people. He wants us to be lifeguards, not umpires.

When Jesus was teaching in the temple, the Pharisees brought in a woman who had been caught in adultery. The Pharisees wanted her to sin no more. To them, that meant judging her sin and giving her what she deserved according to the law — death by stoning. Jesus also wanted her to sin no more. But He offered her life so that she could live in righteousness.

Both Jesus and the Pharisees were trying to accomplish the same thing. But one resulted in death and the other in life.

Many people who are living in the tree of the knowledge of good and evil believe they are doing the right thing for God. But they can lose sight of the big picture and the ultimate goal to abide in and manifest the life of God. I see this happen all the time in raising children.

Training Children in the Tree of Life

Most Christian parents have a great deal of appreciation for the mercy of God, and they live in the tree of life. But when it comes to raising their children, they change it into a value system based on their knowledge of good and evil. So they raise their children accordingly, and their children resent it — unless the children stumble onto the tree of life themselves. Some do, but not nearly as many as we would like.

I know of a wonderful couple who had two easy-to-raise sons. Then they had a strong-willed daughter and didn't know what to do with her. They tried to keep her in line with their knowledge of good and evil, but she rebelled. It wasn't until she was in a Christian rehabilitation program that the parents realized how they had raised their daughter in the tree of the knowledge of good and evil but had never directed her to the tree of life. Now they are so grateful that they and their daughter have discovered the life of God instead of a set of religious regulations.

The Scriptures say, "Train up a child in the way he should go, and when he is old he will not depart from it" (Prov. 22:6, NKJV). "The way he should go" does not refer to our understanding of good and evil. Instead, the way children should go is a lifestyle of seeking life; then they will not depart from it.

Bitterness and Forgiveness

When people are angry or bitter and living in unforgiveness, they have slipped into the tree of the knowledge of good and evil. They have passed judgment on a difficult situation and have decided who was good and who was to blame.

Being right does not necessarily bring you into life. As a matter of fact, being right is practically irrelevant and sometimes counterproductive if it's poisoning you, making you bitter or destroying your freedom in prayer. So you may be technically right — dead right.

After Adam and Eve ate from the tree of the knowledge of good and evil, the shame and embarrassment caused them to blame one another. Adam said Eve was to blame. Eve said the serpent was to blame. Immediately they displaced their personal responsibility and hid from their best friend — God. That's exactly what happens to us today if we react to circumstances based on the tree of knowledge — we end up blaming others for our failures and hiding from God.

Whenever we start blaming others for our own actions or situations, we are really declaring their lordship in our lives. When we blame others we are saying, "God, You are not in charge of my life any longer. Eve is, or the serpent is, or my circumstances are, but You are not."

When you say, "I can't concentrate when I pray. Every time I try to pray, I think about George and the thirty thousand dollars he stole from me. I hate him," you might as well go ahead and say, "George is my lord." You have abdicated authority in your life to someone who has wronged you. You have taken on a victim mentality.

If you are in this kind of situation with anyone or anything, plunge back into the tree of life before the knowledge of good and evil kills you. The tree of life says, "Forgive them. Release them. Trust the Lord." You may still need to take some action, but it must be from a pure heart. If you don't have a pure heart, it would be better to be wronged than to take action. Why? Because forgiveness and trusting the Lord will bring life to you and to those around you.

When you choose the tree of life and refuse to be controlled by the knowledge of good and evil, it disorients demonic strategies. They can't manipulate reactions that come from the tree of life, so they can't develop situations that can control and distract you.

As a matter of fact, it disempowers human enemies, as well, when you live in the tree of life. Some people intentionally try to make us angry or bitter. Often they want us to hate their enemies with them. But when we choose to stay in the tree of life, it keeps us free from ungodly control.

I often talk with people who have been wronged and other times with people who explain why they hurt someone else. Both sides always want my support, but I have decided never to take on anyone else's offenses. Furthermore, if these people start to become bitter, the condition of their hearts becomes more threatening than the original wrong. That's why Jesus said to turn the other cheek, go the second mile or give your cloak as well.

Justice doesn't demand that we protect the life of God in our hearts. Instead justice says, "Argue your point. Win over your enemy. Prove that you're right. Win!" Life, though, thrives on mercy and forgiveness. God knew that the knowledge of good and evil would kill us, so we must consciously choose actions that foster life.

As Christians, we have only one enemy, and he is the devil. No human being on earth is our enemy. If we are convinced that somebody is our enemy, we need to love that person, forgive him, pray for him and be so gentle and kind and loving that Satan can't get his claws into us.

Tree of Life Warfare

Living in the tree of life is lifestyle warfare. It tears down the kingdom of Satan and promotes the kingdom of God with every decision we make.

Why do we praise God?

Because it stimulates His life in our lives.

Why do we attend church? Why do we treat people with kindness? Why do we forgive? Why do we turn the other cheek? Why do we give tithes and offerings? Why do we care for the poor? Why do we reject offenses?

Because it stimulates His life in us and others.

Why do we avoid hatred? Why do we avoid immorality? Why do we refuse drugs?

Because they promote death in us and those around us.

Remember: In the tree of life, we are to do the things that bring life to people, including us.

Finally, let's apply tree-of-life thinking to our city. Think what would happen if we attempted the five primary principles according to the tree of the knowledge of good and evil. We would get angry at ourselves and other people anytime we didn't do them right. We'd be arguing with each other and blaming whomever we felt was "the problem." As a result, the five principles would be much less effective at changing the spiritual climate of the area.

But when we live out the five principles from the tree of life, our hearts don't become dark if mistakes are made. That's because our motivation is not to execute the principles perfectly. It is simply to bring life to the people around us.

God told Joshua: "I have set before you life and death, blessings and curses. Now choose life" (Deut. 30:19).

The Natural Result: Innocence

The first thing I look for when considering a new staff member is innocence. If a person conveys innocence, I know they understand living in the tree of life.

Jesus addressed the need for an innocent heart when He said, "I tell you the truth, unless you change and become like little children, you will never enter the kingdom of heaven" (Matt. 18:3).

Jesus loved innocence. He seemed to be chuckling when He said, "I praise you, Father, Lord of heaven and earth, because you have hidden these things from the wise and learned, and revealed them to little children. Yes, Father, for this was your good pleasure" (Matt. 11:25-26).

115

What was the Father's pleasure? To reveal spiritual truths to humble people who had a simple, heartfelt love for Him. I am convinced that this verse explains why so many are so knowledgeable, but lack the freedom and power in life to demonstrate genuine anointing.

Childlike innocence is easy to identify. An easy laugh, a quick smile, instant forgiveness and a wholesome sparkle in the eye all mark those who protect their innocence. It's easy to be friends with innocent people. And it seems as if those who understand innocence easily cultivate long-term relationships, an effective prayer life and a special anointing in the Holy Spirit.

But negative relationships and the injustices of the world are constantly trying to steal our innocence. They are constantly trying to make us angry, bitter, resentful, greedy or hateful. Jesus knew that His disciples would have to deal with wickedness, just as we do. So His instruction to them included the protection of their innocence when He said, "I am sending you out like sheep among wolves. Therefore be as shrewd as snakes and as innocent as doves" (Matt. 10:16).

How are we supposed to appropriate and maintain innocence?

1. Live in the tree of life, not in the tree of the knowledge of good and evil. When we make our decisions and evaluations from a tree-of-life perspective, the natural by-product is innocence. As we protect the innocence God so freely gives, the next natural benefit is the free operation of the fruit and the gifts of the Spirit.

2. Walk in forgiveness. Everyone of us has opportunities to be hurt, disappointed, rejected or offended every day. If we allow those events to cause us to resent others and think negatively of them, then we can no longer serve them effectively or represent the gospel to them. I believe we need to forgive them weekly, or in some cases daily, in order for innocence to remain dominant in our lives.

3. Discern the root of bitterness and reject it at all costs (Heb. 12:15). People become bitter for a reason, but those reasons are never as terrible as the bitterness that follows. Whether the bitterness is growing in us or in someone we know, we must make sure that it is dealt with immediately. In order to protect my innocence, I never take on someone else's bitterness. To keep from doing this, I won't let people talk to me if they are attempting to cause me to be bitter along with them. I'll pray with them, but if they insist on keeping their bitterness, I'll try to redirect them toward a positive course of action. If that doesn't work, then I'll reconsider the closeness of our relationship until they can forgive.

4. Let love cover the sins of others. Love means that we will do what's best for another rather than what's best for us. Many times, in order for us to maintain our lives and the lives of others in the tree of life, we must let "love cover over a multitude of sins" (1 Pet. 4:8) and intentionally "keep no record of wrongs" (1 Cor. 13:5). I've found that the best way to do that is to be willing to forget other people's failures or problems, be willing to pray about situations and never talk to others about them, and simply mind my own business. In other words, there is an honorable role in acting as if we don't know too much, though there are certainly times when this course of action is not possible. I need to understand that my role is not to cause everyone to fit into my understanding of what is good or evil about them, but rather my role is to keep myself and them growing in the tree of life, thus protecting the innocence of both of us.

5. Practice verbal spiritual warfare. During times of prayer it is important to commune with God and confront demonic influences. I believe that binding and loosing are an important part of protecting innocence (Matt. 16:19). For example, you may need to bind selfishness, self-pity, greed, inferiority and arrogance and loose love, concern for others, giving, confidence and humility. Address demonic influences as quickly as possible, and loose the ministry of the Holy Spirit. That way you will flow in the refreshing that is offered through the life of the Lord Jesus.

The enemy hates it when we live in the tree of life and protect our innocence. His goal is to seduce us into making our decisions based on our knowledge of good and evil, which makes us victims and causes us to blame others. Once we blame others for our negative situations, those whom we blame become our lord, and the enemy has accomplished his goal — death. In Christ we do not need to be victimized in any way, nor do we need to victimize anyone else. But should we ever accept victimization — the immediate consequence of being dominated by the sinful nature — the world and probably demonic influences will consume our lives.

Life is better than knowledge of good and evil.

Innocence is better than victimization.

The ministry of the Holy Spirit is better than the acts of the sinful nature.

There is great power in innocence. According to Proverbs 21:8, "The way of the guilty is devious, but the conduct of the innocent is upright." In innocence we find freedom to pray, socialize with others and minister to anyone. Innocent people don't need to avoid others, hide anything or be ashamed or embarrassed. Instead innocence fosters boldness, life, joy and inspiration. Innocence is always the natural by-product of an encounter with life.

In order to accomplish our primary purpose. we must have the innocence to work with a broad variety of people and institutions. So in order to accomplish our primary purpose, we must choose life and protect our innocence. Then the opportunity exists to make it hard to go to hell from our cities.

Ten

PRACTICING FORGIVENESS

Power Point #2

We hesitate to forgive when we are offended because we are sure that the other person is wrong. Forgiveness has nothing to do with who is right or wrong. Nor does it mean that we condone what that person did. It simply means that we will not let another person's sin ruin us. Forgiveness prevents someone else's action from producing hurts, wrong attitudes or sickness in us.

Forgiveness is the natural result of living in the tree of life. It will bring life to us and to the person we forgive. But spending our time contemplating who is right or wrong only leads to death. The person in the wrong is condemned, and the person in the right feels victimized. No one wins.

Bitterness

When we stop forgiving, we open ourselves to hatred, bitterness, malice, resentment, jealousy, pride and a long list of other problems. One of the most destructive of these negative attitudes is bitterness.

The book of Acts gives us a practical illustration of the effects of bitterness. In Acts 8:9-25, a man called Simon the sorcerer, a cultic magician, offered money to the apostles in order to buy the power of the Holy Spirit. After Peter rebuked Simon, he identified the man's true spiritual problem: "I see that you are full of bitterness and captive to sin" (Acts 8:23).

These two conditions, bitterness and sin, always go hand in hand. Because of Simon's bitterness, he was unable to understand the spiritual depth of what he saw Peter doing — praying for people to receive the baptism in the Holy Spirit. Everything Simon saw became distorted in his mind. As a result, he was unable to grasp eternal events clearly.

The same thing happens today in someone who becomes bitter through failure to forgive. As bitterness makes him captive to sin, a clear perspective of life and spiritual realities becomes impossible.

Physical Illness

I do not believe that every problem or sickness is the result of an unforgiving spirit. But people do actually become physically ill because of bitterness and unforgiveness. Consequently, dramatic healings sometimes take place after confession of long-standing resentments.

When someone wrongs us, we need to release that person to the Lord and forgive so that we can receive freedom to grow in Christ and fulfill God's plan for us. It's in our best interests to trust God, forgive others and let the Lord defend us.

120

Life to Those Around Us

After we forgive someone for offending us, the door is also open for God's Spirit to work in that person.

An excellent Bible example of this principle is Stephen and his attitude toward those who were stoning him to death. While they were hurling the stones, Stephen said, "Lord, do not hold this sin against them" (Acts 7:60). This forgiving attitude released the grace of God to work in the hearts of the very people committing the offense. One of those people was a man named Saul who desperately needed that grace. As history records, God's grace transformed Saul into Paul. The conclusion of that world-changing story is known to us all.

This biblical principle is vitally important for believers to understand. The offended Christian must release the offender to God, or the grace of God won't have the liberty to work in the offender. Trusting Jesus as defender is true faith.

Let me give you a personal illustration:

Several years ago a woman in a nearby church started spreading vicious, untrue rumors about me. The effect of her gossip was far-reaching and negatively impacting people to whom I was trying to minister. She was sweet and cordial to me in my presence, but when I was absent, she slandered my life, work and activities.

As I thought about how to confront the situation, I decided that I needed a clean heart first. Each evening I went for a walk and told God I forgave this woman. Although her stories grew worse and I was deeply offended, I was determined to be clean inside before I confronted her. So I continued my evening declarations of forgiveness.

Then one night God dropped genuine forgiveness into my heart. By His grace I had actually come to love the woman. Now I was no longer emotionally involved with what she said. I was ready to deal with her when God opened the door. To my amazement, once I released her through forgiveness, I didn't have to confront her. God did it for me. I haven't heard one wicked word from her since.

Jesus is our defense! Jesus is our protector! Jesus is faithful!

Jesus is also the best example of a forgiver. When we all turned our backs on Him while He hung on the cross, He opened us to God's grace by saying, "Father, forgive them" (Luke 23:34).

If we want to open the door for God to influence people in a powerful way, forgiveness is the most effective method. Jesus taught it, Paul practiced it, and experience demonstrates it. Forgive.

Keeping Your Heart Clean

Jesus encourages us not to enter into personal conflict or arguments over temporal issues such as money, houses, clothing or personal pride. Why? Because our hearts can't handle it. As soon as we enter into personal debate with "enemies," we find that our natural responses to fight, worry and become bitter take precedence over our spiritual concern to liberate people from bondage. Our perspective moves from the eternal to the temporal, and we risk losing the victory Jesus provides.

Because Jesus understands these natural tendencies, He gives clear instructions about how we are to handle our enemies. He said, "Love your enemies and pray for those who persecute you" (Matt. 5:44). Why did He say this? So our hearts will stay clean. That's why He tells us, "If you are offering your gift at the altar and there remember that your brother has something against you, leave your gift there...go and be reconciled to your brother; then come and offer your gift" (Matt. 5:23-24).

Jesus also knows the devastation that can occur in the heart of a person in willful conflict with another over temporal things.

Settle matters quickly with your adversary who is taking you to court. Do it while you are still with him on the way, or he may hand you over to the judge, and the judge may hand you over to the officer, and you may be thrown into prison. I tell you the truth, you will not get out until you have paid the last penny (Matt. 5:25-26).

Notice that the Lord does not promise justice if we are in the right. He doesn't even seem concerned about who is right and who is wrong. Instead He indicates that the person listening to His teaching will lose, and that the primary goal must be to settle the matter quickly. Jesus knows these conflicts are futile and that they pollute our hearts. If we trust Him and obey His Word concerning our enemies, be assured that He can defend us.

The enemy (Satan) works to produce hatred in the heart of the Christian. Because of his schemes, we must determine never to let any other person ruin our lives by making us hate them. If anyone succeeds at making us hate them, then we have lost our innocence and our life. But when we love our enemies and pray for those who persecute us, we block the plan of the devil and open the door for the ministry of the Holy Spirit in our hearts as well as in the lives of others.

The apostle Paul, quoting from the book of Proverbs, wrote: "If your enemy is hungry, feed him; if he is thirsty, give him something to drink. In doing this, you will heap burning coals on his head" (Rom. 12:20). Contrary to popular belief, the "burning coals" are a blessing to the person. Fire was an important commodity in Bible times. People transported it by moving coals, sometimes carrying them in a container on their heads. So to heap burning coals on their heads was to give them a valuable and practical gift as an expression of love.

This point probably was demonstrated best by Jesus Himself. When the whole of humanity became His enemy, He still gave them His best gift. And it is because of this demonstration of love for His enemies that we are able to serve Jesus today.

Effective Prayer

The effectiveness of our prayer life is strategically linked to our relationships with others. Jesus told us, "When you stand praying, if you hold anything against anyone, forgive him, so that your Father in heaven may forgive you your sins" (Mark 11:25). People often lose their desire to pray when they are hurt or wounded. Why? Because they instinctively know that their prayers are hindered by either their unwillingness or inability to forgive.

Only one biblical solution exists, and that is to forgive. God's Word clearly teaches that we are not to fight these battles. He is. But in order for Him to be effective, we must make determined efforts to obey His Word· "For we know him who said, 'It is mine to avenge; I will repay,' and again, 'The Lord will judge his people'" (Heb. 10:30).

The same thought is repeated in Romans 12:19: "Do not take revenge, my friends, but leave room for God's wrath, for it is written: 'It is mine to avenge; I will repay,' says the Lord."

When a person becomes a Christian, he loses many of his rights. One of them is the right to hold a grudge. Paul writes forcefully about forfeiting our rights: "I have been crucified with Christ and I no longer live, but Christ lives in me. The life I live in the body, I live by faith in the Son of God, who loved me and gave himself for me" (Gal. 2:20). Paul here reveals a critical secret to successful Christian living — dying to self.

How to Forgive

Many people tell me they would like to forgive, but they

have been so deeply offended that they can't forgive. In such situations it may become necessary to engage in spiritual warfare against demonic powers that might keep you bound to unforgiveness. (I address this in my booklet *How to Take Authority Over Your Mind, Home, Business and Country.*) In these instances you must stand against demonic spirits and attitudes of unforgiveness, bitterness, rage, disappointment and other influences that keep you miserable. Evil spirits must be cast out, attitudes renewed by God's Word and the Holy Spirit of God given freedom to work in order to obtain a genuine spiritual victory.

As you pray, declare your forgiveness every day to the Lord. As you do this over a period of time, God's grace will break through that tough exterior produced by hurt and grant genuine forgiveness in your heart.

Force yourself to forgive. Don't wait for it to happen naturally. It won't happen. You must take control in the name of Jesus. Each time you do this, God will honor your obedience and fill your heart with forgiveness. Greater freedom in your prayer life will result, and the Lord will greatly develop your spiritual potential. I recommend that you study the following Scripture verses before going through the prayer of forgiveness.

Mark 11:25	Prov. 25:21-22
Luke 17:4	Matt. 5:44
Eph. 4:32	Matt. 7:1-2
Luke 6:28	Lev. 19:18
Col. 3:13	Prov. 20:22
Prov. 24:17	John 20:23
Eph. 4:26-27	Eph. 5:1-2

Prayer of Forgiveness

Heavenly Father, in the name of the Lord Jesus Christ, I have a confession to make. Instead of loving certain people

I have resented them and have unforgiveness in my heart toward them. In obedience to Your Word, I rebuke a spirit of unforgiveness, rebellion, grief, sorrow, hurt, self-centeredness and pride and command all related spirits to loose their grip on my life.

In the name of the Lord Jesus Christ I now forgive. . (List all people, living and dead, who have disappointed, hurt, offended or wounded you in any way. Also list any organizations or groups who have hurt you. Parents, be sure to forgive your children by name if they have hurt you by not fulfilling your expectations of them. Also, forgive them for being ungrateful and so forth.) I release all these people in the name of the Lord Jesus Christ.

Lord, I ask You to forgive all of them, too. In addition, I forgive myself for my sins and shortcomings and ask You to heal my wounded spirit. In Jesus' name, amen.

Eleven

BECOMING A SERVANT

Power Point #3

In Jesus' day the Jewish nation lived under the control of a contingent of Romans who exercised ruthless command over the Jewish citizens. Those controllers were under the dominion of fewer people in Rome, and over those people ultimately came one person, Caesar, who had great power and influence.

This type of control system is typical in society — from the playground to the corporate boardroom. You could diagram it as shown in Illustration 8 on the following page.

There are groups of people controlled by a smaller group of people who are controlled by an even smaller group. Ultimately this leads to one influential person who has a

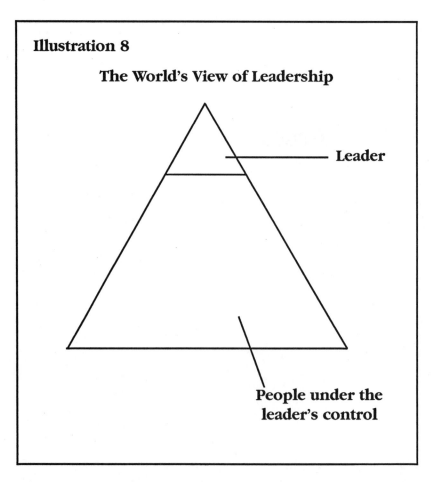

Illustration 8

The World's View of Leadership

Leader

People under the
leader's control

great deal of power over others. Jesus' disciples bought into this power scheme and thought that following Him gave them control over others.

They actually argued about who would be the greatest in Jesus' kingdom. Jesus turned their ambition upside down when He said, "If anyone wants to be first, he must be the very last, and the servant of all" (Mark 9:35).

The mother of two of the disciples even got into the power play. She came to Jesus and asked Him to place her sons in senior positions of authority when He established His kingdom (Matt. 20).

Jesus told her she didn't know what she was asking for. When the other ten disciples heard about the request, they were indignant. Jesus responded:

> You know that the rulers of the Gentiles lord it over them, and their high officials exercise authority over them. Not so with you. Instead, whoever wants to become great among you must be your servant, and whoever wants to be first must be your slave — just as the Son of Man did not come to be served, but to serve, and to give his life as a ransom for many (Matt. 20:25-28).

Jesus frustrated those who wanted Him to climb to the top of the "power and influence" pyramid. Illustration 9 represents Jesus' attitude toward people. He was working His way to the bottom so He could serve the most people.

When Jesus entered Jerusalem, the Jews were convinced that the time had come for Him to overcome the Roman authorities and the corrupt Jewish rulers who had cooperated with the Romans. They ran into the streets shouting, "Hosanna to the Son of David! Blessed is he who comes in the name of the Lord!" (Matt. 21:9).

They knew He could work miracles.

They knew He was articulate.

But He didn't cooperate in overcoming the political power of the Romans.

He didn't work any miracles during His trial.

He didn't give any clever answers to overcome the authorities.

Instead He appeared powerless and remained speechless. The people turned against Him and called for His crucifixion.

When Jesus allowed Himself to be crucified, many people were convinced that He was not the coming ruler they had anticipated. But He died to serve mankind. Then He rose from the dead and ascended to the Father's right hand, where He is today, making intercession for us — serving again, as Lord of all.

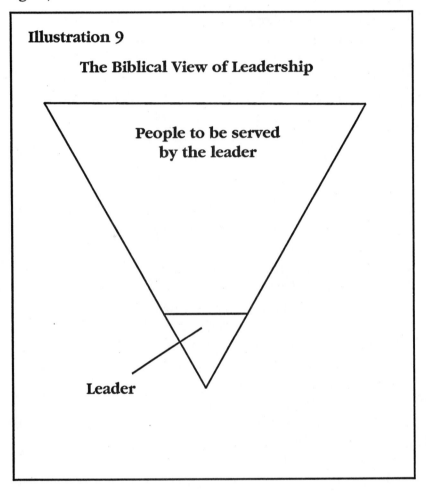

Illustration 9

The Biblical View of Leadership

People to be served by the leader

Leader

The Philippians 2 Attitude

Paul understood Jesus' point about servanthood: to be great in the kingdom of God, you strive to serve the most people. He wrote:

Do nothing out of selfish ambition or vain conceit,

but in humility consider others better than your-selves. Each of you should look not only to your own interests, but also to the interests of others.

Your attitude should be the same as that of Christ Jesus: Who, being in very nature God, did not consider equality with God something to be grasped, but made himself nothing, taking the very nature of a servant, being made in human likeness. And being found in appearance as a man, he hum-bled himself and became obedient to death — even death on a cross! (Phil. 2:3-8).

To be like Christ, we obey to serve. I call this the Philippians 2 attitude.

- Why do we pray and fast? To gain His power in our lives so we can serve others.

- Why do we read our Bibles? To grow in Him so we know how to serve others.

- Why do we attend church? To worship Him with our fel-low believers so we can serve one another and the lost.

- Why do we give tithes and offerings? To honor Him and demonstrate, in a tangible way, our concern for others.

- Why do we pray? To commune with Him and to con-front the schemes of the enemy, so we can be a bless-ing to others.

- Why do we brag about the Lord? To bless the Lord and to strengthen ourselves and encourage others.

- Why do we live holy lives? To demonstrate that God has changed us and to gain the respect of others so they will allow us to serve them.

- Why do we keep our word? To reflect the nature of

the Lord so others will know we are genuine, thus giving us opportunity to serve them.

- Why are we faithful spouses? So our marriages will reflect Christ and His church, opening the door for us to serve others.

- Why do we need growing churches? To serve others.

- Why do we have budgets? To care for others.

The Philippians 2 attitude affects every aspect of life in a positive, powerful way.

Servants Change Hearts

Life is full of joy when you look at it as an opportunity to serve others. A guest from out of town visited our church for a week and a half. I asked her what she thought of our church, and she said, "You all sure are nice to each other."

"Why do you say that?" I asked.

"Well," she replied, "every time I walked into the church offices, someone asked if they could get me a drink. When it was time for lunch or dinner, two or more people volunteered to get me something to eat. People at your church obviously enjoy treating each other well, and it spilled over into serving me."

That's a Philippians 2 attitude.

When the churches of Colorado Springs were participating in the Christmas gospel ad campaign, we got a phone call from a blind woman whose seeing-eye dog had just died. She told the phone counselor, "I don't need to get saved as much as I need a new dog."

We found out what kind of dog she needed, went out and bought one, and delivered it to her the next week. I believe that is what Jesus would have done. Making sure that woman received a new dog was the greatest possible sermon she could have ever received. She didn't pray with us to receive Christ immediately, but her heart opened as she saw people taking care of her in Jesus' name.

The Salvation Army, Compassion International and every local church whose members take food to a grieving family or provide a ride to an elderly person or mow the grass for someone who can't do it themselves demonstrate the mind of Christ — the Philippians 2 attitude.

In the ten-year history of New Life Church we have had only one fight. It wasn't over the design of a building, the leadership of a class or a budget question. Instead it was between two women who were fighting over the same vacuum cleaner. They both wanted to serve the church on that Monday morning. I went out and bought another vacuum.

Harmony is unusual because the world trains us to try to control, manipulate, protect our territory and fight for the top. But when we choose to serve, we confuse demonic schemes because we become unpredictable.

Satan loves to lie to people and say that Christians are no better than anyone else. He capitalizes on the failures of high-profile Christians. But his lies sound hollow when nonbelievers find themselves being served by Christians with no ulterior motives — just a desire to serve.

This attitude is obvious when you are uniting for your primary purpose in a city. A humble spirit from a servant's attitude causes others to have an open heart toward you. If your attitude reflects your desire to bless them and cause them to be successful with no ulterior motives or sinful manipulation in mind, people will welcome you and open their hearts to you. So we become more effective when we work toward the bottom instead of the top.

Twelve

SHOWING RESPECT

Power Point #4

Another Christian in town decided that he wanted to start a church in his home after New Life Church had been functioning for about a year.

He didn't consult his neighbors or embrace a respectful attitude toward those in authority. Soon the neighbors started complaining about traffic. This brother fought his neighbors, fought the city and ended up in several legal battles trying to defend his church.

By the time the struggle was over, he left the city in the middle of the night angry at other churches, his own parishioners and the city. This brother sincerely thought he was fighting for righteousness, but he didn't help the secular community at all in its understanding of the gospel. Instead he actually made it more difficult for the kingdom of God to expand.

If this incident had happened before we started New Life Church in my home, it would probably have caused my neighbors to be excessively cautious, and they would never have let me do it.

Consideration of others goes a long way. I don't believe that we could ever underestimate the power of respect. But while saying that, I recognize that it's not always easy to be respectful — especially in major conflicts.

David's refusal to disrespect King Saul, even though Saul was trying to kill David, is a powerful picture for all of us. Further, Jesus demonstrated respect for the Roman government by paying His taxes, and Paul apologized for not showing respect to the high priest, Ananias

Even in the most difficult personal struggles, being respectful toward others helps keep you and the others involved in the conflict living in the tree of life.

Currently, our community is dealing with a government raid on a small Christian boys' ranch near Calhan, Colorado. As time passes, authorities are discovering that the allegations against the ministry were false and that overzealous social services employees violated the civil rights of the ministry, the parents and the students.

There may be numerous lawsuits as a result of this unnecessary government action, but I am encouraging all the Christians involved to operate with respect for authority, no matter who is right and who is wrong.

If parents of the boys or the ministry file lawsuits, the lawsuits must be pursued simply to correct a governmental mistake; they must not be "to get even." They should do it from a heart's desire to serve our community by establishing a legal precedent restricting the authority of the department of social services. But if they want to sue to demonstrate their ability to win over social services arrogantly, then they would not be reflecting a godly lifestyle.

The thousands of prayers about this situation would be hampered if the primary people involved became disrespectful. But when the people involved embrace respect toward others, it becomes a great weapon of spiritual warfare. It negates the enemy's opportunity to portray the Christians negatively and facilitates the ministry of the Holy Spirit.

Spiritual Warfare

Respect denies the enemy a foothold and fosters the types of relationships that can actually gain ground for the kingdom of God. Therefore, it is spiritual warfare.

I believe we are to respect specific authorities God has delegated in four areas:

1. Family
2. Workplace
3. Government
4. Church

I believe that too often our actions negate our words and our prayers and hurt our ability to touch our cities. We believe that the most important thing we do as Christians is to have good church services. But if we don't understand the significance of issues like the power of respect, people won't care about our church services. They will believe that we are hypocrites unless we live a respectful lifestyle.

Family Dynamics

Our ability to foster healthy relationships within our families is a direct indicator of our relationship with the Lord. First Timothy 3:4 and 5 tie the qualifications for eldership with the attitudes and behaviors of our children, and in 1 Timothy 5:8, Paul writes, "If anyone does not provide for his relatives, and especially for his immediate family, he has denied the faith and is worse than an unbeliever."

It is in the home that we learn to maintain long-term relationships, which is God's desire for His body. The disciplines necessary to maintain a healthy family are many of the same required to build integrity within the body of Christ.

Workplace Ethics

God has also placed most of us in a position where we must submit to authorities within the workplace. First Timothy 6:1 and 2 speak about the employee-employer relationship. My paraphrase of this text allows cultural application. "Anyone who works for someone else for their living should consider their supervisors worthy of full respect, so that God's name and our teaching may not be slandered."

Here the Bible directly connects respect for our "bosses" with evangelism. In other words, the Bible indicates that the lifestyles of those who call themselves Christians determine the validity of the message in the minds of their co-workers and associates.

Government Validity

In 1 Timothy 2:1-4, the Bible is very clear regarding our responsibility to pray for those in authority over us. In doing so, God will grant "peaceful and quiet lives in all godliness and holiness" (v. 2). In Romans 13:2 Paul equates our attitude toward governing authorities with our attitude toward God: "Consequently, he who rebels against the authority is rebelling against what God has instituted, and those who do so will bring judgment on themselves."

Local Church Relationships

I believe relationships in a church are like relationships in a family — you need to build them on respect and plan for them to last. One of the great failures of the modern American church culture is the way we encourage pastors to relocate from church to church every few years. I understand that there are some benefits, but the costs are much higher. Our local churches exist for specific purposes, and those purposes hinge on the integrity of healthy, long-term relationships. When we move our pastors often, we deny them the opportunity to learn through long-term relationships. And both the church and the pastor learn the skill of short-term, superficial relationships that are actually counterproductive.

In the church we see the long-term effects of a respectful lifestyle. It is hoped that as a family raises children in a church, they will know the same people for decades. In this environment we learn that loose speech, undisciplined behavior and a haughty attitude will destroy long-term relationships. But when respect is practiced, long-term relationships become natural, and the church community easily prospers.

Earn the Right to Be Heard

Two men from the Middle East operate a local Oriental carpet store here in Colorado Springs. They are both Islamic. One day my wife and I went in to purchase some carpets, and these men and I became friends. After a long conversation they discovered that I was a "priest." Because of the decency of our conversation, they immediately started asking me extensive questions about God. They were very interested.

Now our friendship is over a year old, and every time I am near their store I stop by, and we have wonderful conversations. I am confident that these men have developed

138

great respect for both the gospel and Christians. I may lead them to Christ one day and baptize them, but even if I don't, I'll always respect them.

I believe that people are the way they are for a reason and that my role as a Christian is to treat them with respect. I tell myself to treat people as if I would need to ask them for help in the future (though I'm certainly not planning to!). Everyone is important, and as people are treated with dignity, their hearts become open to the message of our lives.

Pray for Those in Authority Over You, Then Trust Them

I encourage you to make a list of those in authority over you in each of the four areas outlined earlier and pray for those people regularly. In addition, make a list of those under your authority that you are responsible to protect. Pray for them regularly, acting as a faithful prayer shield.

Then start seeing everyone you deal with from the perspective of respect. Even if the situation seems negative, treat people respectfully. With that, the five principles will have greater effectiveness in your city.

13

Cultivating Character

Power Point #5

We have all seen the gospel message maligned because of the actions of someone who claimed to be a Christian. I am convinced that many who have rejected the gospel don't actually have a problem with the gospel but with the character of the individuals proclaiming it.

The successful accomplishment of our primary purpose rests only in part on our methods of proclaiming the gospel or in our prayer lives. I believe its foundation lies in successfully earning the right to be heard because of our personal character.

I preach several times a year at New Life Church about the kind of message we send to nonbelievers through our character. Paul told the Thessalonians, "Make it your ambition to lead a quiet life, to mind your own business and to work with your hands, just as we told you, so that your daily life may win the respect of outsiders and so that you will not be dependent on anybody" (1 Thess. 4:11-12).

Paul puts it in very practical terms here: If nonbelievers don't respect you, they are not going to listen to you. And you earn respect through the character you live out every day.

A friend of mine works at a company where there are very few Christians. The one Christian in her department is a man whose work habits are exceptional. He is respectful and pleasant. He is never pushy or arrogant, but helpful and nice. Because of his character he has earned the right to be heard, and through this he has opened the door for the expansion of the kingdom.

If we pay our bills on time, leave generous tips for waitresses, serve our families faithfully, support our churches and forgive grudges, others will be more open to us. Think of it this way: Our character can be a deciding factor in somebody else's salvation.

The Bible ties character and spiritual warfare together in Ephesians 6, where Paul describes successful spiritual warfare by the wearing of the armor of God. Each piece of the armor points to personal character.

The Belt of Truth

Telling the truth and wearing a belt do the same thing: They keep the important things in our lives in the right place.

When wearing the belt of truth, we don't do privately what we would be ashamed of publicly. Probably the easiest way to put on the belt of truth is to live by the motto: "There is no such thing as a secret."

If you want to keep something secret, don't tell it. If you

want to do something and you think certain people will never know, don't do it. As soon as we believe that we can think, say or do secret things, there is a greater opportunity for the enemy to persuade us to violate God's Word. After all, the newpaper's best headlines are accounts of people doing things they thought would remain a secret.

When David met with Bathsheba "secretly" and had her husband killed "secretly," he never dreamed those secrets would be discussed openly for thousands of years. When Judas developed a "secret" code to identify Jesus with a kiss, he never thought that code would become the most notable event of his life.

Joseph Stalin, Adolf Hitler and Pol Pot most likely thought their great public achievements would earn them places in history as great leaders. Instead their "secret" activities are what they are remembered for — the murders of millions of their own citizens.

One more thing about the belt of truth: It is not an exhortation to say everything we know. The Bible exhorts us to use wisdom and discretion in our speech, so it would be foolish to say anything and everything that goes through a person's mind. Our words are to be honest but wise.

Remember: There is no such thing as a secret.

The Breastplate of Righteousness

Several years ago a pastor friend of mine had to inform three children that their father had decided to divorce their mother and had left with another woman. When the children heard the heartbreaking news, they became so upset that they were physically sick to their stomachs and vomited. Why? Because the father removed his breastplate of righteousness. It made his own heart vulnerable to deception and, at the same time, caused the hearts of those who trusted and loved him to become vulnerable.

The purpose of a breastplate is to protect a person's life-giving organs from damage. Righteousness protects the hearts of our friends and relatives from the wounds that would be caused by our unrighteousness. Righteousness makes long-term, healthy relationships possible.

None of us lives an independent life. Our decisions affect others. When a spouse is unfaithful or a parent violates the innocence of a child, the resulting hurt can be spiritually life-threatening.

One of the easiest ways the devil gains a foothold into a believer's life or family is through unforgiveness, bitterness or anger. These reactions are sparked by the pain of unrighteous acts: betrayal, immorality or some other violation.

Living a righteous life not only keeps our own conscience clean but protects all of our loved ones for generations to come. The blessings of righteousness or the consequences of violation extend for generations.

If our relationships are not rooted in righteousness, we, in effect, invalidate our own prayers. Our prayers and our lifestyle must go hand in hand. Why? Because both are spiritual warfare; both hinder demonic activity and enhance the opportunities of the Holy Spirit.

Several years ago a woman called me excitedly to say that she had led her neighbors to the Lord and that they would all come to church together on Sunday. When Sunday came, she was there alone. She told me that on Friday night she and her neighbors had celebrated their newfound salvation by getting drunk together; then she slept with the husband. The family was angry at her and wouldn't have anything to do with God, the church or her. What was so amazing was that she didn't understand what had gone wrong.

Her lack of righteousness contradicted her witness so strongly that any positive decisions made by her neighbors were negated and she potentially did more harm than good.

Remember: Live a lifestyle that protects people's hearts.

Feet Fitted With the Readiness That Comes From the Gospel of Peace

This piece of armor is simple. We need to go to the places our purpose in Christ demands us to go. Let your "feet" be Spirit-dominated and obedient to God's Word, free to go where the gospel asks us to go.

Where we choose to go or not go is powerful spiritual warfare for us and others. When we attend church, a Bible study or some other wholesome activity we are strengthened in godliness and, just by our presence, strengthen others. Prayer walking, taking a prayer journey, visiting someplace nice with your family or enjoying a Little League baseball game with your child enhances the Holy Spirit's opportunity for ministry.

Conversely, if someone visits a prostitute, an adult bookstore, a bar or a meeting promoting anti-Christian attitudes, that person gives the devil a foothold in his or her personal life and, simply by being there, encourages others in sinful activities. When we neglect the maintenance of our homes and avoid family and church activities, we are in effect hampering the Lord's work in our hearts and the hearts of others.

Britt Hancock, the senior intercessor for Freedom Ministries, and I took three days to pray and fast in downtown Colorado Springs. During that time we walked through the downtown area on prayer walks — taking special time for government buildings, churches, adult bookstores and bars.

When walking around many of the adult bookstores, we were surprised that we didn't sense much demonic activity. Then we noticed a pattern: When several people were in the bookstore, we had to battle spiritually while praying over the bookstore. But when the bookstores were empty, there seemed to be very little resistance.

Demonic activity is sometimes involved with inanimate objects and places. But the ultimate goal of all demonic power is to influence the activity of people. So we concluded that the number of people in the bookstore determined the intensity of the demonic activity involved.

One time while walking through an adult bookstore parking lot we noticed a car with a Christian bumper sticker. I left a note on the car offering assistance to its driver if he would like to call. We waited discreetly for a few minutes to see how the note would be received.

A young man who appeared to be a college student came out of the bookstore and glanced around apprehensively, obviously feeling guilty. He looked embarrassed as he read the note on his car; then he drove away quickly.

He was probably a struggling Christian. He apparently didn't like what he was doing. But by being in the wrong place he was feeding the wrong spirits. His "feet" were not Spirit-led.

I have learned that after men like this one sin, they go through extended times of guilt and remorse. They repent fervently and then, sometime later, repeat their sin.

This young man would have accomplished his goal if he had prayed with his actions as well as his words. He should have confessed his struggle to an older, strong brother and visited a place other than the bookstore. Avoiding the bookstore would have been a more powerful act than an extended time of prayer before or after.

The places we choose to go and the places we avoid have direct spiritual significance. Sometimes by our presence we possess places for the kingdom; other times we should avoid certain places at all costs. But the lifestyle principle is important for all Christians to understand. Thoughtfully determining where our feet take us is spiritual warfare.

Remember: Let your purpose in Christ determine where you go.

The Shield of Faith

During times of prayer and fasting, the Holy Spirit will plant His vision for our lives, our families and our cities in our hearts. Carrying the shield of faith means that you are walking with such confidence in God's vision for yourself and your city that the fiery darts of the enemy don't even arrest your attention.

When my phone rings late on Saturday nights and someone threatens to kill me the next morning during church, I unplug the phone, roll over and go back to sleep. When I observe intensive spiritual struggles within our congregation, I just keep praying, preaching the Word and loving them — just as I normally do — and we stay steady in the midst of the storm.

Less than a year ago, the church janitor arrived early one Sunday morning and saw evidence that witchcraft incantations had been performed directly outside our front door during the night. He knew my policy on that so he prayed quietly, cleaned up the mess and didn't tell me until Wednesday. We prayed and talked, went to lunch and kept serving people and never told the congregation about it. Why? Because it's a distraction.

During one of my out-of-town trips, my wife, Gayle, received numerous threatening phone calls from a local warlock. The last one she received woke her from a deep sleep right at midnight. It involved a lengthy rhyming incantation which ended with "Tell all of this to Ted." Still somewhat groggy, all she could think of to reply was, "Is that all?" The caller slammed down the phone, and she went back to sleep. That was the last time we heard from him.

The shield of faith frustrates our spiritual enemies because we appear to be apathetic toward them; we give them no respect. In reality we are concerned about them and their spiritual influence; but when they take shots at us, we just raise our shield of faith. (By the way, Satan's most effective "darts" are not necessarily occult intimidation. They can be burnout, sin, wasting time, focusing on differences in the church, sexual temptation and so on.)

We fight the good fight of faith by diligently, consistently and faithfully fixing our eyes on His mark and pursuing it for the sake of the lost in our city. Then no weapon of the enemy is effective against us, and we have used God's shield of faith.

Remember: Being consumed with His vision leaves no time for distraction.

The Helmet of Salvation

Thoughts precede words, and words precede actions. If a person violates scriptural principles in his thought life, very soon his actions will reflect it.

The helmet of salvation is the disciplining of our thoughts according to the biblical standard. We submit our values and opinions to God's Word and allow His transformation to protect us from the schemes of the enemy.

That's why good books are better than bad books, and good movies better than bad movies. That's also why meditation on the Scriptures is life changing. The helmet of salvation — thinking thoughts "saved" people ought to think — enhances the Holy Spirit's opportunities to use us and thwarts the enemy's schemes. It's a lifestyle of warfare.

Paul wrote to the church in Philippi, "Finally, brothers, whatever is true, whatever is noble, whatever is right, whatever is pure, whatever is lovely, whatever is admirable — if anything is excellent or praiseworthy — think about such things" (Phil. 4:8).

In his letter to the Romans, he again teaches the importance of thinking according to God's plan: "Do not conform any longer to the pattern of this world, but be transformed by the renewing of your mind. Then you will be able to test and approve what God's will is — his good, pleasing and perfect will" (Rom. 12:2).

So to put on the helmet of salvation, we learn the Word of God and think according to His plan. In Romans 8:5-7 Paul writes, "Those who live according to the sinful nature have their minds set on what that nature desires; but those who live in accordance with the Spirit have their minds set on what the Spirit desires. The mind of sinful man is death, but the mind controlled by the Spirit is life and peace; the sinful mind is hostile to God. It does not submit to God's law, nor can it do so."

But how do we start? By applying the blood of Christ to our minds to make powerless the thoughts that can easily cause us to be slaves to sin. Hebrews 9:14 explains the vital work of the blood of Christ in our minds by saying, "How much more, then, will the blood of Christ, who through the eternal Spirit offered himself unblemished to God, cleanse our consciences from acts that lead to death, so that we may serve the living God!"

These passages demonstrate clearly that our success is determined by God's work in our minds, changing the things we think about. If we focus on the obstacles before us, then we will allow those obstacles to dominate our prayers and actions, which will result in our cities remaining in darkness.

Or we may pray, study the Word and put on the helmet of salvation, understanding that God has a plan that needs to be thought about, dreamed about and considered. In that atmosphere the Holy Spirit will do the miracles necessary to change our cities and deny the enemy his ground in our thoughts, our lives and our cities.

Remember: Think the thoughts of an eternal person.

The Sword of the Spirit (The Word of God)

If we don't know the Word of God, any demonic or

worldly idea may seem reasonable. It is, in fact, the Word of God that keeps mankind from believing he is his own god. If our own opinions, thoughts or conclusions are our highest authority, we are in serious trouble because we are capable of horrendous thoughts and, therefore, horrendous actions.

God's Word gives us a standard for genuine character. The Word terrifies every demonic stronghold because it develops in all Christians the ability to wage continuous lifestyle warfare.

We have two interdependent sources of discovering the Word of God — a personal relationship with Jesus Christ, the living Word of God; and the Bible, the written Word of God (see Heb. 4:12 and John 1:1-2). Both encourage growth in the other.

From the Bible we discover God's great vision for us, our families, our cities, our nation and our world. Through communication with Jesus, we learn tangible methods of negating the world's power and thwarting demonic schemes. These two dynamic forces communicate God's will and methods. When used appropriately, they are always successful.

The information in the Bible is alive. It speaks directly into our situations and gives specific guidance. It teaches us how to keep the snares of the enemy and the failures of our own pasts from entangling us.

That's why we pray the Word of God, sing the Word of God, speak the Word of God, meditate upon the Word of God and long to be saturated with the Word of God. It is the sword that transforms us from pacifists to activists, from introspective thinkers into city changers, from people pleasers into persuasive promoters of His kingdom.

Remember: The Bible is the basis of authority in all of life

Pray in the Spirit

Throughout the centuries, volumes have been written

about the effectiveness of prayer that is dominated by the Holy Spirit. In a brief description of his own prayer life, Paul revealed in 1 Corinthians 14:14-15 two ways of praying: with the mind and with the spirit.

Praying with his mind means that he was praying in his native language or at least in a language that he understood in the natural. These are the prayers commonly spoken in group meetings in the church or before a meal. When praying in an understood language, we trust that our prayers are highly influenced by the Holy Spirit and that praying in a known language can be "praying in the spirit."

Paul also identifies prayer in another language, or "tongues." In 1 Corinthians 14:2 he writes, "For anyone who speaks in a tongue does not speak to men but to God. Indeed, no one understands him; he utters mysteries with his spirit." I believe tongues, then, are a way believers may pray in a language that they have not learned naturally.

Millions of believers worldwide have experienced praying in tongues. From 1 Corinthians 13:1 where he notes, "If I speak in the tongues of men and of angels," we can conclude that when people pray in tongues their spirits may be speaking to God in an earthly language from some other place or time, or they may be speaking in an angelic language. But this we know for sure: When they pray this way, they edify themselves (1 Cor. 14:4), their prayers are the perfect will of God (Rom. 8:27), and their faith is strengthened (Jude 20).

Why should people pray in tongues? The book of Romans suggests that the Holy Spirit helps us express ourselves to God.

> In the same way, the Spirit helps us in our weakness. We do not know what we ought to pray for, but the Spirit himself intercedes for us with groans that words cannot express. And he who searches

our hearts knows the mind of the Spirit, because the Spirit intercedes for the saints in accordance with God's will (Rom. 8:26-27).

Praying in tongues is biblical but is not an end in itself; its purpose is to edify the believer so the believer can serve others.

Giving the Devil a Foothold

Throughout this chapter I have talked about how putting on the armor is living a lifestyle of character, and that character denies the devil a foothold in your life. That principle comes from a key passage in Ephesians 4:27: "Neither give place to the devil" (KJV). This passage in Ephesians is surrounded with practical teaching about character, such as speaking the truth, controlling anger, earning a living, fleeing from sexual sin and avoiding drunkenness.

Faults in character will give the devil a "place" in your life that he will use to destroy your ability to fulfill your primary purpose. It doesn't matter how spiritual you seem to other people. You won't fool the devil, and you won't fool God.

Remember: There is no such thing as a secret.

14

PRAYING FROM HEAVEN

Power Point #6

When Ronald Reagan was an actor living in California, communist leaders had no fear of his views, even though the actor had strong opinions about the threat communist countries posed to the free world.

Then *actor* Reagan became the *president* of the United States. As president, he jokingly tested a microphone one day by saying, "Five, four, three, two, one — we just bombed Moscow." Those words caused a major international incident. Not because Ronald Reagan the ex-actor said them, but because Reagan, the president of the United States, the one man on earth in a position to initiate a major nuclear attack on the Soviet Union, had said them.

Position

The positions we hold indicate the authority we can exercise. After the "We just bombed Moscow" incident with the president, I was at church testing one of our new microphones, and I jokingly said, "Five, four, three, two, one — we just bombed Moscow." Absolutely no one cared. No bombers took off. NORAD didn't heighten its alert status. Ambassadors in Washington and Moscow weren't alarmed. Why? Because it didn't matter what I said. I didn't hold any political or military position. I wasn't the president.

Understanding our position is vital. A nineteen-year-old young man becomes a representative of his nation when he puts on the uniform of his country's armed services. He is still the same young man, but the uniform indicates his position. The man may enjoy certain freedoms and liberties as a citizen, but when he is in his uniform, his behavior must reflect a different standard — because of his position.

We believers are required to embrace our position in Christ if we expect to become successful in prayer and action for our cities. I remind myself: always pray from heaven, never from earth. Let me explain what I mean by "praying from heaven."

Our Position in Christ

In the beginning verses of Ephesians 2, Paul talks about the remarkable changes that have occurred in all who believe.

As nonbelievers, we were slaves to sin, bound by the world and victimized by the "ruler of the kingdom of the air, the spirit who is now at work in those who are disobedient" (Eph. 2:2). Then in verse 6 he says, "And God raised us up with Christ and seated us with him in the heavenly realms in Christ Jesus."

So when we became Christians, our position changed to one of being at the right hand of God, in Christ Jesus, co-laboring in His kingdom. We were no longer under the authority of evil spirits on earth.

When I pray against demonic strategies, I must fully understand the reality of my position in Christ.

Personal Demonic Strategies

During the summer after my freshman year of college, I went home to Yorktown, Indiana, to spend the summer with my family and friends. One evening I went to Yorktown Baptist Church, the church instrumental in leading me to Christ, and entered the empty auditorium to pray.

No one else was in the building so I was just relaxing and walking around casually fellowshipping with the Lord when I felt as if I were seeing something unusual. Since I had heard about people having visions in the Bible, I knew they happened during times of prayer, so I sat down in one of the empty chairs and continued praying.

I saw a delivery room where hospital personnel would bring women who were having their babies. Hovering over the delivery table, I saw a series of dark spirits of various sizes and shapes. One seemed to be in charge, and the others were waiting for his command.

As women were brought into the delivery room to give birth, the lead demon would assign one of the subordinate demons to each newborn baby. To one he would assign alcoholism; to another, sexual perversion; to another, religious arrogance; to another, the distraction of wealth or power. Some babies were assigned demons who would entice them toward fear, greed, hatred, self-consciousness, confusion, rebellion or foolishness. As a nurse carried the baby, and the mother was wheeled out, the demon assigned to the baby would accompany them.

From that vision I thought I gained insight into the seriousness of the devil's schemes. I could immediately identify in my own life the probable scheme the enemy would like to use to prevent me from achieving God's best for my life. I wanted to test the validity of my conclusion, so I also asked other people, "Can you tell me the one primary way the enemy would like to destroy you?" In practically every case the person questioned gave me a specific, immediate response.

As people go through life, they have opportunities to succumb to a variety of temptations, and several of them may be encouraged by demonic forces. Even though I believe that Satan will use specific demons to tempt individuals, that fact is not an excuse to give in to the temptation. Demonic schemes must be resisted just as temptations that come from the flesh are resisted.

You can resist demonic schemes by refusing to surrender your mind to sinful thoughts, refusing to act on sinful desires and welcoming the Holy Spirit in your life.

Prayer is also a powerful weapon against the demonic scheme in a person's life. An average person who is not the recipient of Christian prayer may be unduly influenced by demons of hatred, lust, greed, self-pity, deceit, pride and so on.

I believe these demonic spirits linger, waiting for an opportunity to become directly involved in a person's life. Should that person give them a foothold and learn to cooperate with them, then the person may become demonized.

Just as demons have wicked plans for individuals, so I believe more powerful ones have assignments to infect entire communities. If they thought about it, most Christians can describe the strategy that Satan uses to pollute their communities. But they may not realize that these strategies are executed by evil spirits that specialize in certain kinds of sin and deceit. A city may be targeted by a spirit of lawlessness, occultism, greed, perversion, control, pride, poverty and so on.

The purpose of these territorial spirits is to prevent the manifestations of God's kingdom, to paralyze the Christians and to promote their own evil nature through the lives of people within their territories.

According to Ephesians 1:21, Jesus has been given power over all "rule and authority, power and dominion, and every title that can be given, not only in the present age but also in the one to come." I am convinced this passage describes Jesus' authority over demonic spirits that desire to destroy people's lives.

So as we pray from our position in Christ in heaven, we also have authority over demonic powers through Christ. I want to describe for you the spiritual dynamic that I believe happens when we pray against demonic activity.

Christian Prayer Stimulates the Holy Spirit's Activity

As we pray for someone, our prayers always stimulate the Holy Spirit's activity in and around the person for whom we are praying. They also diminish the freedom of evil spirits that are hoping to gain additional influence over that person. Illustration 10 shows the change in a person's environment when he is the recipient of another's prayers.

As we pray for people, we have the authority to alter the spiritual environment they are living in, but we do not have the authority to dominate their personal will. They are still responsible for their own choices. But if they are being prayed for, their opportunities to receive positive spiritual input are greatly increased because demonic influences are displaced by godly influences of either the Holy Spirit or angels. As we pray for individuals, the potential of their being able to respond positively to the gospel greatly increases.

The same is also true of the places we pray for. As we pray for our cities, the spiritual climate can be altered as evil spirits are removed and the blessings of God come. A community that has been prayed for has a much higher response to a gospel presentation than a community that has not received prayer. Illustration 11 is a picture of the changing spiritual climate of a city as believers pray.

Illustration 10

The Impact of Prayer on an Individual

Hatred

Self-pity   Lust

Pride   Anger

Individual Harassed by Demonic Influences

Confidence   Love   Purity

Self-pity   Hatred   Lust

Humility   Peace

Pride   Anger

Individual With Demonic Influences Neutralized by Prayer

Illustration 11

The Impact of Prayer on a City

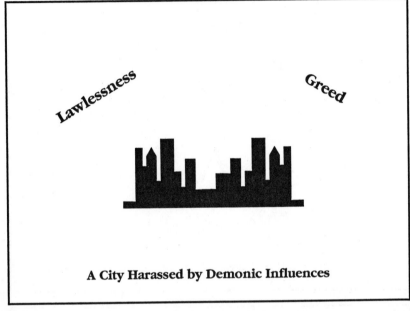

A City Harassed by Demonic Influences

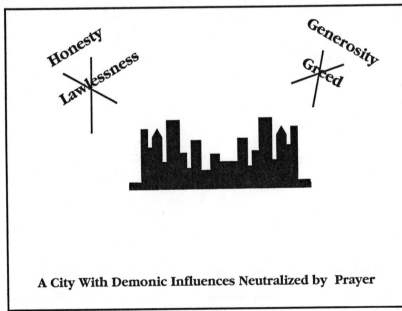

A City With Demonic Influences Neutralized by Prayer

When effective Christian prayer is absent, the heavens are closed and demonic/worldly influences are dominant. But when Christians start praying, the demonic influences can become so weak that a vacuum actually develops and the kingdom of God can be manifested with greater effectiveness. In these places, massive conversions, life-giving church growth, societal improvement and great spiritual encouragement occur.

It's not hard. A little prayer goes a long way, and a lot of prayer does even more, because prayer stimulates the Holy Spirit's activity and thwarts demonic activity.

This is also a very effective way to pray for leaders in society. For example, if we pray for the Senate, it obstructs the opportunities of evil spirits to suggest thoughts and ideas to our senators and facilitates the chances for the Holy Spirit to give them ideas. As we pray for our Congress, president, police force, schoolteachers, pastors and others, the same is true.

Christian prayer always diminishes the influence of demonic powers and stimulates the ministry of the Holy Spirit. It always works. It never fails. But we can't take any position on earth and expect effectiveness. Instead we must pray from our position in heaven at the right hand of God in Christ Jesus, because only in Him do we have authority.

Always Pray From Heaven

Paul drives this point home in Ephesians 3 when he writes: "His intent was that now, through the church, the manifold wisdom of God should be made known to the rulers and authorities in the heavenly realms, according to his eternal purpose which he accomplished in Christ Jesus our Lord" (vv. 10-11).

The world, the devil and his demons do not want people to understand the realities of the gospel. It is the god of this world, Satan, that works to blind the minds of those who

159

don't believe. And no one can come to an understanding of the gospel unless the Holy Spirit reveals it supernaturally. Consequently, there is a massive spiritual struggle on the enemy's part to keep people blinded to the gospel.

God has chosen, though, to enforce the freedom available through the gospel, through the church — through you, the believer. And that is the role of confrontive prayer. In prayer we 1) gain life through communion with Him, then we 2) use the position of authority in Jesus to make known the perfect will of God to demonic rulers and authorities. That's violent, confrontive prayer. It's not hard; it's not complex; nor is it mysterious. It always works when Christians do it. But it's not sweet — it's violent.

This is something only we in the church can do. There is no other group that can provide an environment of spiritual freedom that opens the door for people to respond to the gospel. Only we in the church, by praying from our position in heaven, can diminish demonic influences and stimulate the Holy Spirit's activity.

15

COMMUNING WITH GOD
AND CONFRONTING THE ENEMY

Power Point #7

L ord, I'm starving," I prayed one time after three days of prayer and fasting. I was taking a walk through a forest in the foothills of the Rockies and decided to tell God just how much I was suffering for Him.

"I am hungry for a Big Mac, a chicken leg, some corn or mashed potatoes and gravy," I moaned. "Please, God, I'm not playing anymore. I may be dying. I want a chocolate shake, a loaf of bread, anything Chinese or Mexican. My pulse is rising, and my breathing is shallow. I might not live much longer. I have to have some food."

After grumbling about my hunger some more, I smiled and said, "Lord, I want You to know something. I'm really

nungry for some food — but I'm even more hungry for You."
Then, He smiled.

A Date With God

I think of prayer and fasting as having a date with God.
It is a specified time set aside for me to spend time with
Him and for Him to spend time with me. I usually go for
three days with a Bible, some juice and water, a tape play-
er and tapes, and great excitement.

When my friends ask me how to get started I say: "Do a
juice fast your first day, a water fast your second day and
juice again on your third day. I've found that keeps me alert,
energetic and sharp so I can walk, pray, study or whatever
I need to do while fasting. You might not enjoy it too much
while you're fasting, but the results will be worth it when
you're finished."

As you seek the Lord, abandon yourself in prayer. Pray
until you press past your personal concerns and become
consumed in His power. Push through your personal suffering into His. Pray and fast for three days, and you'll
receive new ideas, refreshment, liberation and strength.
With that, then, prepare for spiritual victory.

While praying and fasting, the enemy will try to perform every
trick to paralyze you. He will try to trick you into excessive
analysis or suggest that negative spiritual developments
should be blamed on someone else. He will do all he can
to distract you or cause you to fail. So keep it simple. Fast,
pray, read your Bible and let the Lord work in your life.

As you do that, God will give you ideas to help you man-
age your time, reorganize your priorities, eliminate your
secret sins, conquer distractions in your life, and rethink failure and success. He will give you the wisdom necessary to
keep you out of church politics and focused on purpose.
He'll teach you about rejection, hurt, passion, family and
finances. In the atmosphere of prayer and fasting, God will

work miracles in your body, mind and spirit.

I try to fast three days every month. While praying and fasting, we become more spiritually sensitive — to both types of spiritual activity. So as you commune with God, become saturated in the Scriptures and fellowship with the Holy Spirit, you will also have opportunity to put off the flesh and confront demonic activity. In that environment the absolutes of the Scripture come alive with the revelation that the absolutes are our message — because they are the fundamentals of successful Christian living. When our spirits are active, the absolutes are well-defined.

While praying and fasting, God will give you thoughts on how to minister His Word to people not usually exposed to the gospel. Your intellect will become increasingly available to the Spirit, so ideas will flow freely as you seek the Lord and pray for those in your city. In this setting ask God for a revelation of His love for the lost of your city. Ask Him to show you heaven and hell. Read the Scriptures regarding eternal life and eternal destiny.

And let His transformation take place. Let the love of Christ compel you and the terror of the Lord motivate you. Embrace the necessity of raising the water level of the Holy Spirit's activity. Life-giving churches will grow, and new ones will be planted so thousands may come to Him. Pray for this process in your city so that strong, stable believers and life-giving local churches serve the people of your city.

In order to stay alert, I sometimes go on prayer walks through communities while praying and fasting. Other times I spend the time seeking the Lord and listening to Bible tapes. Fasting is a catalyst that the Holy Spirit uses to do a quick work in our lives. I believe the ministry of the Holy Spirit and the message of the Bible come alive during such times. Praying and fasting increase my spiritual authority, create humility, provide rich opportunity for personal spiritual warfare and allow time for rest: constructive solitude — time to think.

I have never known one person with an addictive behavior who has been permanently set free without developing a lifestyle of prayer and fasting. The same character qualities are necessary to pray and fast that are required to live a life pleasing to the Lord.

We have a choice. We can learn to discipline our bodies and live a Spirit-filled life in the seclusion of prayer and fasting, or let the Lord teach us those lessons in public, which may be embarrassing. I choose prayer and fasting. In it we learn about communion with God — knowing Him — and confrontation — denying the flesh and standing firm against the enemy's schemes.

In Luke 4, the Bible records Jesus' forty-day fast. During that time He obviously had tremendous encounters with God the Father, but He also had at least three major confrontations with the devil.

That is exactly the nature of our prayer times — both when we are fasting and when we are not. I believe that about 85 percent of our time in prayer should be spent fellowshipping with the Holy Spirit, communing with the Father in Jesus' name, praising and worshipping Him and getting to know Him. Conversation with Him, knowing Him and communicating with Him are the essence of our lives in Christ.

But that is not all of it. We also need to confront the enemy and his schemes. In the midst of confrontation we may verbally combat the enemy using the name of Jesus or specific Scripture verses. Confrontation is a vital part of what we do in prayer.

Confrontation

Ground-Level Spiritual Warfare

"Pastor Ted, I need you to pray for me," Mrs. Grayson said with concern in her voice. "My family is in trouble because my little girl is out of control." She told me the story of her nine-year-old daughter, Susan*, who had been on medication for several years and was having to spend more and more time in the hospital. There was no consensus among her doctors about her specific diagnosis, but her mother was sure that schizophrenia was her illness.

"My daughter is so unpredictable. She seems so nice but then becomes so aggressive. What can we do? We don't want to lose our daughter!"

As she sat in my office crying, I asked her a number of questions trying to determine if the daughter's problem was indeed a mental illness or if she was struggling against evil spirits.

After our conversation the mother decided that she herself needed prayer. I agreed and offered to pray for her right then. She wanted deliverance.

As I prayed for her, she sat calmly with her eyes closed and her hands folded. Nothing seemed to be happening. After we finished, she thanked me cordially, and we walked together into the reception area.

The church secretary was anxiously waiting for us. She said Mrs. Grayson's husband had called several times but finally decided he couldn't wait for a return phone call. He was on his way to the church right then with Susan.

Mr. Grayson, like his wife, seemed very composed. Their daughter was pleasant. After all three came into my office, Mr. Grayson said, "Susan went into a trance about an hour ago and started saying things that didn't make any sense at all. She would say, 'Don't pray that. I hate you,' or 'I don't care what you say. I'm not coming out.' Another time she said, 'You are wicked. This is where we've lived for years, and you aren't going to make us move.'"

As he told us what she said, Mrs. Grayson and I both realized that Susan was responding to the prayer I had just prayed over her mother. I had never heard of such a thing.

---

* The names used in this story have been changed to protect the privacy of those involved.

I asked Susan if she would work with us in prayer to see if the Lord would heal her mother and her. She looked at me with hope in her eyes and agreed.

Over the next few months this family learned spiritual warfare. I gave them my warfare prayer booklet, *How to Take Authority Over Your Mind, Home, Business and Country,* so they would have enough information to pray effectively at home. They came to the office weekly, and we prayed and counseled together for an hour or so. After a few months, Susan no longer needed any hospital care, and her doctor was experimenting with reduced medication. After six months Susan was off her medication, enrolled in school and becoming involved in church.

The Scriptures authorize us to liberate captives (see Is. 42:7; 49:9; 61:1), but too often we want to believe that we can do God's work without confrontation. I don't believe the biblical model of ministry allows us that luxury.

Dr. C. Peter Wagner, in his book *Warfare Prayer,* calls individual deliverance "ground-level spiritual warfare." I believe deliverance ministry is so important that it is the responsibility of every Christian to know how to cast a demon out of a demonized person. (If you feel as if you don't know how to cast out a demon, look at the examples Jesus gave in the Gospel of Mark.)

Dr. Wagner also describes occult level confrontations with demonic activity. Occult level warfare negates demonic activity stimulated through the occult. For example, occult-level spiritual warfare would be needed in a situation where an occult curse brought demonic attacks into a person's life. I also believe we can pray against demonic resistance that often comes against church bodies as a whole.

Practically every Saturday night when I go to the church to pray for the upcoming Sunday services, I pray to cancel the spiritual power of any negative words or actions that have advanced against our church body, the families of our church and my family in particular.

I believe individuals, families and churches should regularly practice occult-level spiritual warfare because there is no way to know what others are trying to do to you spiritually.

Strategic-Level Spiritual Warfare

Strategic-level spiritual warfare is the third level of warfare described by Dr. Wagner. Strategic-level spiritual warfare is confrontational prayer that affects demonic powers that influence entire regions.

When we pray for a region, we assume our position in Christ at the right hand of the Father and use that authority to pray for the spiritual climate of the entire region. That type of praying is effective anytime at weakening demonic principalities and blessing people.

Sometimes we travel to key locations or places of spiritual power in order to pray on site. High places overlooking a city or spiritual power points in a city are effective spots to pray strategically against territorial spirits. These power points are considered to be places that strengthen the demonic activities of your region or city, like a particularly popular bar, cult-type church or occult worship site. Sometimes particular government buildings, Masonic lodges or old religious sites are power points.

In October 1993 I led a team of thirty-one people on a prayer journey to pray strategically for Albania. While there we had three vivid experiences in which members of our team experienced strategic-level spiritual warfare. One of those occurred when I accompanied three others to a cave in the side of a mountain where a local Islamic boy had told us demonic activity was taking place.

Fifteen hundred years earlier a man went to the top of this mountain to pray because he was so burdened by his sin. While praying, he realized that he needed an atonement for his sins. This grieved him terribly. In the midst of his sin and because of his lack of knowledge, he entered a large cave in the side of the mountain and killed himself, hoping to make atonement for his own sinfulness.

That cave has been a place of animal (and maybe human) sacrifice ever since.

Our guide led us to the narrow stairway built into the face of the cliff leading to the cave. We saw drops of fresh blood shimmering on the stone steps. The guide was so frightened as we neared the entrance of the cave that, as soon as he had pointed out the place we were looking for, he took off. The rest of us realized that this high place had become an evil stronghold centuries earlier and we had to do all we could to neutralize the demonic activity.

As we walked down into the cave, we noticed a pair of shoes at the entrance, characteristic of a place of worship in Eastern countries. Because of the shoes, we realized that one of the worshippers was still present from the morning sacrifice. Upon entering the worship area, we noted Islamic religious symbols distorted by their makers into satanic symbols. (I had seen the same type of distortions in American satanism, except that in America they use Christian or Jewish symbols and distort them.)

As we walked and confronted demons in the name of Jesus, we came to a dark cavern with dozens of candles on the floor and ledges. In fervent confrontational prayer we prayed that only the God of Israel — the God of Abraham, Isaac and Jacob — would be worshipped in this place. We took oil, a symbol of the Holy Spirit's ministry, and placed it on the candles and on the walls darkened by hundreds of years of smoke.

As we prayed, we sensed that waves of freedom were pouring into the cave, but to be effective we had to find the place of sacrifice.

With our adrenalin flowing and our senses alert because of the unusual combination of fear and confidence, we passed through the worship area to see another branch of the cave that went even deeper into the mountain. Upon entering we saw four covered altars and, just beyond them, an underground spring. We immediately felt great fear and waves of terror. We were praying, thinking, worrying — and nervously watching for the worshipper we thought was probably hiding in a crevice somewhere.

We confronted terror with confidence in being His ambassadors. We overcame anxiety from the obvious danger with thoughts of serving people by liberating them from demonic religious manipulation. Fear came and went. But faith was always there.

Cheri Will, a homemaker and intercessor, and I started breaking curses, anointing altars with oil, driving demons out of the cave and asking God's glory to fill the place in Jesus' name. Vince D'Acchioli, one of our church elders, stayed near the entrance with Tina Perez, a children's worker from church, and prayed for our protection. We realized that God was doing a great miracle.

As terror subsided and confidence increased, we left the cave wondering why we never located the owner of the shoes at the entrance. By now the blood was dry on the steps. As we walked away from the cave, we saw a group of nationals who had gathered at the top of the mountain and were running about and yelling. They were telling people excitedly that a group of Americans had come to drive the demons away from the cave.

In the midst of joy and excitement, though, at the pinnacle of the mountain stood a small woman in a black dress, pointing at us with one hand and spinning her demonic prayer wheel with the other. We saw her and began praying for her and walking toward her. She ran away from us toward a wooded area while continuing to spin her prayer wheel.

While Vince and I diverted the attention of the nationals who had gathered, Tina and Cheri went to the top of the hill and prayed for God's blessing and mercy to come upon the people of this region. That is strategic-level spiritual warfare.

How do we know the prayer journey to Albania was effective? According to reports we have received from numerous sources, the body of Christ there grew 600 percent from October 1993 to October 1994. There were many reasons for that growth, and the size of the body of Christ in Albania is still extremely small. But Albanians now willing to accept the gospel is one indicator that prayer has been, and continues to be, effective.

As you pray for your city, it is important to consider what territorial spirits may be trying to hinder the growth of God's kingdom in it. Very simply identify those spirits and use the authority you have in Christ to weaken or remove those demonic principalities. In your hometown, that prayer is prayed two ways: 1) through verbally confronting demonic strongholds and praying for God's kingdom to be established and 2) by a lifestyle that expresses your faith.

Thy Kingdom Come

Obviously, praying for the manifestation of the kingdom of God in people's lives must be the desired result of all intercession. Before and after times of spiritual confrontation, communion with the Father is very necessary. Often I pray the portion of the Lord's prayer that says, "Your kingdom come, your will be done on earth as it is in heaven" (Matt. 6:10).

This portion of the prayer is particularly powerful in praying for the people in our cities. When we pray for God's kingdom to be established in people's hearts, we are asking that His Spirit work in their lives.

I take three primary lists from the Bible — the seven spirits of the Lord (Is. 11:2), the fruit of the Spirit (Gal. 5:22-23) and the gifts of the Spirit (1 Cor. 12:7-10) — and pray that they will be manifested in the lives of the people of my city. I know that the fruit and the gifts can only be fully manifested in the lives of believers. But I know that they are also blessings in nonbelievers' lives to whatever degree they can operate.

When praying for others, ask God to give them these blessings. Taking the time to study each of these subjects will enhance your fervency as you pray, "Your kingdom come, your will be done on earth as it is in heaven." These are the evidences of the kingdom of God in people. Pray that God will give them:

Isaiah 11:2

- The spirit of the Lord
- The spirit of wisdom
- The spirit of understanding
- The spirit of counsel
- The spirit of power
- The spirit of knowledge
- The spirit of the fear of the Lord

Galatians 5:22-23

- Love
- Joy
- Peace
- Patience
- Kindness
- Goodness
- Faithfulness
- Gentleness
- Self-control

1 Corinthians 12:7-10

- Message of wisdom
- Message of knowledge
- Faith
- Gifts of healing
- Miraculous powers
- Prophecy
- Distinguishing between spirits
- Tongues
- Interpretation of tongues

As you are praying, look over these lists and ask God to give these things to the people of your city. Ask for "the Spirit of the fear of the Lord" to minister to everyone in your city. Pray for God to send self-control and faithfulness to the people of your city. Think of the results when you pray for the Spirit of prophecy to come upon all the government officials of your city or the message of wisdom to work through every judge and jury in your city. Pray for every police officer to distinguish between spirits. (I believe simply praying for Colorado Springs police officers has contributed to the increased effectiveness of our police department.)

We pray that God will give every citizen faith. Their increased confidence in God because of faith will prepare them to receive the gospel. We need healing in our hearts, miraculous powers to protect our children, and goodness and faithfulness in every home.

"Your kingdom come, your will be done on earth as it is in heaven."

Everything on these lists is evidence of His kingdom. Everything on these lists is His perfect will. Everything on these lists allows a little slice of heaven on earth.

OUR RESPONSIBILITY
TO PRIMARY PURPOSE

16

HEAVEN OR HELL?
YOUR CITY. YOUR CHOICE.

E ach morning our church receptionist places a copy of the obituaries from the morning paper on every church staff member's desk. Attached is a post-it note that says:

Today from Colorado Springs people will go to heaven, and people will go to hell. The percentage of people going to heaven and the percentage of people going to hell today is determined by how well you did your job yesterday.

If you remember heaven today, it will help someone else avoid hell tomorrow.

Why do I do this? Because we all need to be reminded constantly of our primary purpose: to make it hard to go to hell from our cities.

The Bible provides a clear picture of hell. Jesus had an intense concern that people avoid hell because it is where "their worm does not die, and the fire is not quenched" (Mark 9:42-48). When Jesus referred to hell, He often would describe it as Gehenna, which was a burning dump near Jerusalem. Perpetual burning with worms, maggots, fire and trouble — a lake of fire — the absence of life. Remorse and torment are the prevailing emotions. Agonized wailing, the painful grinding of teeth and the endless sizzling of burning human flesh are the prevailing sounds and smells.

Alone.

No way out.

No second chance.

God does not want anyone to spend eternity in hell (2 Pet. 3:9). Hell was prepared for the devil and his demons (Matt. 25:41), so the only people that perish are those who reject God. God doesn't send them to hell; they send themselves by choice (John 3:17-18).

The Church

The apostle Paul lists two major motivations for his effective ministry. One is found in 2 Corinthians 5:11 where he writes, "Knowing, therefore, the terror of the Lord, we persuade men" (KJV). This passage reveals that Paul had a sincere understanding of the horrible nature of the wrath of God and the terror that will come upon His enemies. Therefore he feared for those who did not know the gospel. Paul was consumed with the finality of that reality and, therefore, was motivated to persuade men.

A few verses later Paul writes, "For Christ's love compels us" (2 Cor. 5:14). Then he gives an explanation of the gospel. Here he communicates that he is compelled by the love of

175

Christ for himself and for others. It seems as though Paul had a strong understanding of the reality that judgment is real but that God is deeply in love with mankind. The gospel, then, is the reality that no man needs to pay the price for his own sins but that each one can avoid judgment by faith in Christ Jesus. God is in love with the lost, and that constrained Paul.

The responsibility of that message is now in the trust of you and me, the church. We are the church.

- We are the only ones with the message that guarantees eternal life.

- We are the only ones with unlimited access to God the Father.

- We are the only ones with the power of the Holy Spirit and the authority to negate the influence of demonic strategies.

- We are the only ones who are able to overcome "the gates of hell."

- We are the only ones in our cities who can do His job.

- We are the only ones who are exclusively responsible because we are His body, His co-workers, His ambassadors, His friends.

He gave us His nature, His will, His plan, His Spirit, His grace, His love and His anointing.

Our role as liberators is a life-giving responsibility. Paul referred to this when he said, "I am clear of my responsibility. From now on I will go to the Gentiles" (Acts 18:6; see also 20:26). He was referring to the fact that he had preached to the Jewish people in this region as he was responsible to do; but now that they had rejected the message, his responsibility required him to go to the Gentiles.

176

We at New Life Church pray over each name in the phone book because it is our responsibility to do so. We don't do it for fun or as a gimmick or because it's a novelty. We do it because it may be the difference between life and death. As members of the body of Christ, we are the ones with the authority to remove demonic activity and stimulate the Holy Spirit's activity in the lives of the people of our city. Their therapists are probably nice people, but they can't deal with their demonic problems, their old sin nature or their eternal destiny. But we can.

When we distribute *JESUS* videos, do prayer walks and respect others, we do that for a purpose that only we can perform. We in the body are the only ones who can get people back to the tree of life and have their innocence restored. We are the only ones who can demonstrate that humility overpowers control and manipulation. The church has the power to have genuine character through the armor God gives us. We can commune with God and overcome enemy strongholds — and no one else can.

That's why the Scripture says, "If my people, who are called by my name, will humble themselves and pray and seek my face and turn from their wicked way, then will I hear from heaven and will forgive their sins and will heal their land" (2 Chron. 7:14).

This verse clearly communicates that as we in the body do what only we can do, then that sets the stage for the healing of our land. That is the point of this entire book. We have the resources, the spiritual power and the will of God. Only we can do what needs to be done — make it easy to go to heaven from our cities.

START.

Notes

Foreword

1. "In Colorado Springs Religious Groups Have the Right of Way," *Washington Post,* 25 December 1994, p. A3.

Chapter 1

1. I believe the fulfillment of this was the Promise Keepers meetings of thousands of men that began with Bill McCartney, former football coach of the University of Colorado Buffalos.
2. In 1987, New Life Church helped develop Praise Mountain, a prayer and fasting facility in the mountains of Colorado.
3. Right now New Life Church, C. Peter Wagner (Global Harvest Ministries and Fuller School of World Missions), George Otis Jr. (Sentinel Group) and others are making plans for this prayer center.

Chapter 2

1. Thomas Heath, "In Colorado Springs Religious Groups Have the Right of Way," *Washington Post,* 25 December 1994, p. A3.
2. *Gazette Telegraph,* 27 July 1994, p. A6.
3. Dru Wilson, "New Cattle Mutilations Revive Questions," *Gazette Telegraph* (Colorado Springs), 10 September 1994, p. B6.

Chapter 3

1. This information came from the abstract of votes cast at the general election held on November 3, 1992, obtained from Natalie Meyer, Secretary of State, Colorado Department of State.
2. The teacher took the issue to court and a settlement offer was made. The teacher made a counter-offer which is pending as of January 25, 1995.
3. In fact, an article in the *Washington Post* on December 25, 1994, was headlined "In Colorado Springs, Religious Groups Have the Right of Way." Amendment 2, which brought our city into the limelight, is being challenged in court. It has been rejected by the Colorado Supreme Court as unconstitutional, and the authors of the amendment have made an appeal to the U.S Supreme Court

Other Materials Available
From Ted Haggard

Booklets

Fraud in the Storehouse
So You Want to Get Married?
Freedom Through Forgiveness
No More Lonely Nights
Who's in Charge Here?
Liberation Through Prayer and Fasting

*How to Take Authority Over Your Mind,
Home, Business and Country*

Tape Series

Prayer and Fasting (five tapes)
Obadiah (two tapes)
Prayer Walking (two tapes)
Money (two tapes)
Judges (nine tapes)
Life in Leviticus (nine tapes)
Others: A Study in Relationships (two tapes)
The Philippians 2 Attitude (two tapes)
Marriage: School for Success in Every Area of Life (five tapes)
To Marry or Not to Marry (four tapes)
Focus on the Absolutes (two tapes)
Living in the Tree of Life (two tapes)

The mini-books are available for a suggested donation of
$2.00 each, which includes shipping. For the tape series, the
suggested donation is $5.00 per tape. To order call or write:

New Life Church
11025 State Highway 83
Colorado Springs, CO 80921
(719) 594-6602

ATTENTION PASTORS
AND CHURCH LEADERS

Order *Primary Purpose* for your church
or Bible study group.

Wholesale discounts are available.

Call 1-800-283-8494 for details.

Creation House
600 Rinehart Rd.
Lake Mary, FL 32746
407-333-3132

Recommended Reading

by Dr. C. Peter Wagner
Warfare Prayer
Prayer Shield
Breaking Strongholds in Your City
Churches That Pray
Engaging the Enemy

by Francis Frangipane
The House of the Lord

by Cindy Jacobs
Possessing the Gates of the Enemy

by John Dawson
Taking Our Cities for God

by Steve Hawthorne
and Graham Kendrick
Prayerwalking

by Dick Eastman
The Jericho Hour
Love On Its Knees

by George Otis, Jr.
The Last of the Giants